ANN JAMES

# FOR THE

# LOVE

# OF THE

# HORSE

# VOLUME 1

**AMAZING TRUE STORIES ABOUT THE
HORSES WE LOVE**

*Cover Photo: Epiphany (Odie) and Ann Jamieson*
*In Huntington NY*
*Photo courtesy of: Joel Weber; Beech Tree Images*

*Back Cover Photo: Aljadam and family*


*Volume I revised Format and Design by:*

*Elizabeth Vaculik*

# CONTENTS

## With a Little Help from My Friends

## Surprises

## Beginner's Luck

## The Name Game

## Life has its Ups and Downs

## And More...

# INTRODUCTION

Anyone who loves horses will appreciate this book.

These are all true stories: stories about the bond between horses and humans. That bond is not particular to one breed or one discipline; it encompasses everyone who spends time in any way with these incredibly generous souls.

I wrote this book to celebrate that bond, to honor the horse. Horses bring so many gifts into our lives in so many ways.

This book is a thank you-to my horses, to horses everywhere.

# ACKNOWLEDGEMENTS

Thank you to all my wonderful horses: to Odie and Tucker whose love and goodness have known no bounds. Thank you to Five Star for giving me my first taste of the big time. And thank you to Nicky, Bob, Twilight, and Obi for all you taught me, and for giving me the grace to know that you wanted other careers.

I'd like to thank everyone who believed in this book. Thank you to Hallie McEvoy, for all your help, and the belief that this book had to be published. I want to thank my partner, Richard Sinrod, whose enthusiasm for the book boosted my own. Thanks for all the terrific leads, and for talking to people anywhere, anytime, in search of a story!

Thank you to The Ludwig Vogelstein Foundation, Inc.: your grant at a time when I wasn't sure if I could or should go on proved invaluable, both financially and for the fact that someone believed in my book and my writing ability. People don't believe that grants are really out there-but they are!

I want to thank Betty Oare for always encouraging me. Even when I wasn't writing anything, you kept telling me, "You should be writing. Always keep writing."

Thanks to Hobbes, for sitting in my lap many nights at 3 a.m., keeping me company.

Thank you to my friends Sara Vanacek and Natalia Zunino, who encouraged me and read my stories at many late dinners together. Thank you Natalia, for your suggestions and editing skills, for coming to my rescue when I said "Help! I just can't get this story the way I want it."

Without Sue and Steve Haneman, this book wouldn't be written, for they saved my ailing computer and brought it back to life.

A huge thank you to June Zettelmeyer for reading and editing the entire book.

I'd like to thank all my other friends, old and new, for your support and belief in me.

And a special thank you to all of the owners of these magnificent and generous horses for sharing your stories with me.

# ~⟩ LOVE LETTER TO A HORSE

**D**ear Odie,

Thank you. Thank you for sharing your life with me for 27 years. Whenever I was around you, life seemed easy. Obstacles became small; hurts were forgotten.

You opened my life up in so many ways.

Nature was no longer just a word in a textbook when you came into my life. Together we investigated mountain trails, forded streams, swam in Long Island Sound. On our outings we encountered fox, wolves, snapping turtles, coyotes, white-tailed deer and red tailed hawks, pheasants, bald, and golden eagles. We saw beaver dams and had near misses with skunk families. Otters splashed their tails unexpectedly as we rode by, and then looked amused that we were now (in one leap) at the far side of the road.

We rode through fields of black eyed susans, Queen Anne's lace and daisies, and paused, entranced, at the sight of wetlands bordered by masses of purple loosestrife. A great blue heron that took off from under a bridge we were crossing, flying practically beneath your hooves, spooked us both. And when a wild turkey took off in a thunder of wings from his camouflaged spot beside us, we, too became airborne.

You showed me the meaning of the word generosity. You were only two when we met. I had never trained a horse before, but you showed me what to do. Once you did something the first time, you did it every time and you did it well. You gave so much and were always looking to give more.

Your perfect manners came naturally, When people complimented me on what a good job I did with groundwork, I had tobe honest and give you the credit. I expected other horses to be so good and was never so fortunate.

I watched other people spend hours trying to get their horses on (or off) their trailers. Not you. You self loaded and unloaded. Nobody can deny you had a great sense of humor, like when you walked on the trailer, which had its breastbars down, turned around in the front and with a spunky glint in your eye, walked right out again.

You amazed me with your willingness to help. Gymnastic ability has never been one of my strong suits, so I was not one who could just vault on a horse effortlessly. Nevertheless, I loved riding bareback, so you made it your job to be sure that I actually ended up on your back. Finding whatever rock or piece of wood or mound of grass I could to give myself a little extra bit of height, I would slowly and most ungracefully try to haul myself on. You could so easily have seized the opportunity to meander out of range or move just a little so that I would crash back to earth. Instead you looked at where I was and then chose your position so that I could most easily get on.

Odie, you were so smart. Too smart for me at times. If you didn't want to stay somewhere, you didn't. A double ended snap? Pathetic try. It would hold you for about a nanosecond. Wire twisted around it might at least prove entertaining to you, like humans playing with those tough tavern puzzles. But a deterrent it was not. And if there was too much additional stuff twisted around, well hey, why bother? You just took the gate off its hinges, laid it down and walked out. And took everyone else's gate off their stall, too, just to be sure I got the message.

Paddocks didn't hold you either if you were bored. If you didn't want to be bothered messing with the gate, you would just jump out. Five feet was easy.

You did everything I asked of you and did it well. With

your smooth gaits (riding you truly was like sitting on a cloud) and athleticism, you were pure joy to sit on. Although you were started as a western pleasure horse, you excelled in hunt seat equitation, hunters, dressage, eventing, and hunter paces. Hunting scared me out of my wits, but you found it exhilarating.

Thanks for my first experience in the jumpers, where I bravely clung to your mane and shut my eyes as you leaped over very high, very wide, and very scary fences. If only I'd known then that we had to go through the finish line we would have done well.

You made me a winning partner in hunter paces, introducing me to the greatest thrill I've ever had on horseback: galloping across fields and through the woods like a wild animal, jumping all the inviting fences and sometimes those heart-stopping drops. You were perfect. Blazingly fast, yet you could stop and turn on a dime. Never did we go by an arrow with you on board. If we saw it just as we were about to fly by, no problem. You just did a turn on the haunches at full speed. Were those dressage horses ever jealous. And it didn't take long before you learned to look for the arrows yourself and you would start turning before I even knew what was happening.

Remember that time we accidentally rode onto a movie set? Our normally empty fields were full of people and noise, and brilliantly colored hot air balloons landing all around us.

Yet you didn't miss a beat. After all, those were our racing fields, the place where everyone would come from the barn and race each other. And you, with your racing Quarter Horse heritage, always won. An unbeaten record. Imagine if you'd been on the track? You would have been a rich horse!

And the sunsets we witnessed from those fields. Who could believe the sky could be all those colors? Pinks, purples, oranges, brilliant red, somber gray.

You showed me the joys of the four seasons: the fun of splashing in the bay on horseback, galloping along the beach. Spraying snow into the air as we flew across a wintry field with the moon lighting our way. The feeling of life renewed as we encircled fields of green hay bordered by budding trees. The rapture of a perfect New England autumn, with the glow of sugar maples dressed to the nines in ravishing shades of yellow, orange and scarlet.

Sometimes all I wanted was quiet, and with you I always found it. No matter how taxing school, or work, or life in generaLwas, you could take me away from it all. When my Dad died, and then my Mom, you were there to let me bury my face in your mane and cry my eyes out.

You were opinionated. If you didn't like someone, you wouldn't let them ride you, no matter how accomplished they were. You would hunker down in one spot and refuse to budge. And if they really got after you, well then you'd move all right. Backwards. Fast.

Your bravery was legendary. As a two year old, you crossed bridges, forded streams, climbed over logs, dealt with traffic on the roads and taught all the older horses in the process. When my friend Lany evented you, you finished the cross-country for her even though you were hurt. You slipped and landed on a fence, so Lany stopped and dismounted to look you over. You seemed all right, so she continued. Only when you started hopping on three legs, the moment you crossed the finish line, did we realize something was wrong.

With you I got to do things the "old-fashioned" way, riding home with pumpkins picked from the local patch, dragging a Christmas tree behind you after I proudly cut it down out in the woods (thank God you didn't spook at this thing following you all the way home!), We picked vegetables from a nearby farmer's field and rode home with them in a string bag (carrots for you and cauliflower and brussel sprouts for me).

Thank you for the gorgeous sunny start of spring day when you were so full of yourself that I asked you to use that energy to collect and you did a high, bouncy passage, something I'd never had the pleasure of experiencing before.

Some horses have to actually be taught to stay out of people's space. Imagine. You always knew. I remember that warm day in February when we went out for a bareback trail ride in the snow. We were all in such a good mood, fooled by the beautiful weather that spring was soon to arrive. When Michael told a good joke, I started laughing. I laughed so hard that I literally slid off of you, landing right under your feet. Your right hind foot was already in mid-air, right over me, and there it stopped. And there you kept it until I regained my composure and crawled out from under you.

There was that time at the Caumsett event, when Andy was holding you while Lany got ready. Andy was relatively inexperienced with horses and I'm not sure he wanted to be holding one. It was early morning, the grass was slick and when Andy turned to get something, he slipped, landing right under you. You sat back on your haunches into a levade, and stayed in that levade until Andy, unhurt, was able to get up.

You sure could be wild sometimes, bucking and leaping when I rode you and there was a brisk wind or a chill in the air. But when I got badly hurt, crushed by another horse, you took care of me. You gave me the confidence to ride again, taking each step as though you had precious cargo on your back, never doing a thing to make me fear.

Did I mention how beautiful you were? With your bright copper coat and strapping muscles and the big splash of white on your face. You sure turned people's heads.

Odie, you were such a character. The last show you were in was so typically you. When I rode you in that trail class you were such a brat. Spinning and backing and spooking even though you were 28. Then, a little girl gets on you. It was her very first show and you were *perfect*. Strutted into the ring, won class after class, carrying yourself so big, so proud. The judge loved you. He would have bought you had you been for sale. But you were never for sale. Never. And you made that little girl champion.

For 27 years you shared my life. You got me through all

the bad times: the grief, the long years of Lyme disease, and the times when I was injured. You brought me so much joy and made me so proud.

They say a life well lived is its own reward, but there are rewards for others too. You rewarded everyone who came in contact with you. Thank you Odie. I'll always love you.

# CONNECTION

14

# ⤙ SPIRIT

W hite fluffy clouds puffed lazily by in a cerulean blue sky. Green timothy and alfalfa grew side by side, stirring just a little in the light breeze. Horses grazed in their fields or sunbathed on their sides in the mild sun. It was my day off work, and a perfect day for a trail ride. As I walked up the hill to the back pasture, Tucker, my off the track Thoroughbred, saw me and galloped to the gate. He was as eager as I was to go exploring. I put on his halter and kissed his velvety nose. He gave me a horse kiss and then nudged me toward the gate. "C'mon," he was saying, "Let's go!"

I tacked up quickly. His shiny cinnamon bay coat didn't need much grooming to keep it in show ring condition. The grass, good feed, and his exuberant spirit kept him glowing from within. He danced at the mounting block, piaffing to remind me that his abundant energy needed an outlet.

Up the long hill to the first field we proceeded, basking in the sun and the glory of nature. The past winter had been brutal and long, lasting way into spring. Snow had fallen so steadily that roads had become tunnels, cars barreling through six foot walls of white on either side. People who normally were not snowbirds had been forced to flee to Florida for short breaks just to retain their sanity.

So now, in the early summer, we treasured every ounce of sunlight, every bit of green.

Coming into the first hayfield, which had already been swept clean of its golden green treasure, a young coyote loped out of the woods just ahead of us. He looked at Tucker, and Tucker looked at him, yet neither started. The coyote headed into the cleared field a little above us, and then stopped. He waited until Tucker and I were directly below him, with only about 15 feet separating us. Again, neither one of them appeared at all alarmed by the presence of the other.

Tucker started trotting, and the coyote trotted with us. Then Tucker broke into a canter, and the coyote loped alongside us. Now Tucker turned his head and looked at the coyote. What he said was as clear as day: "Wanna race?"

Apparently the answer was yes, for Tucker stretched out his head and lengthened his stride into that land eating gallop his granddaddy, Secretariat, was so famous for. The coyote responded with a leap into the air and streaked alongside of us. Tucker started to outpace him, and instantly dropped back a notch so that they could continue their game. I was not about to interfere in the moment; I was just a lucky witness to these two magnificent creatures playing on this heavenly day.

We rounded a corner and tore up a hill to where a cornfield lay on our right. The coyote blasted out of sight into the rustling stalks. Tucker stopped, shook his head at the field and pawed the soft ground. The coyote leaped out, and the two took off again, making the lane between the cornfield and the woods into a racetrack. When we reached the end, the coyote again swerved into the waving stalks of corn. Tucker slowed to a walk.

We walked around the far edge of the field, turned at the end, and continued through the next lane. I didn't see the coyote and I thought he was gone for the day. I wondered about him. Where had he come from? What made him come out and join us? He was clearly not sick, for I had witnessed several rabid animals and this pup glowed with health.

Ten minutes later we came out on the farthest edge of the corn, into a cleared grass field. A canine form shot out of the corn and landed less than 10 feet in front of us. The coyote was back.

Tucker stopped and looked at him. "What's up?" I could hear him thinking.

The coyote answered by leaping in the air, jumping up and down and shaking his head, looking for all the world like the family lab wanting to play ball.

"C'mon," he was saying, "let's play! Let's go!"

Tucker responded by developing a sudden infusion of cutting horse blood. Dropping low onto his front end, he swung his head left, then right, shifting his weight to follow the coyote's direction as the handsome canine leapt sideways one way and then the other. This joyful play went on for about five minutes, the two of them totally engrossed in their antics. Then Tucker moved a few feet closer. The coyote jumped forward, narrowing the gap between them to about five feet. At this distance they stopped, and looked at each other. I swear a smile stole across both their faces. Then they cocked their heads at each other, acknowledging one another, and turned to go their separate ways. "Thanks for the dance," they appeared to be saying.

The coyote disappeared into the corn; Tucker and I headed home.

In every living being there is a spirit, a spirit that is connected to all others. When we recognize that, there are no longer any boundaries. In the glory of that remarkable day, I was honored to be part of something far bigger than myself.

# ⌐·⊃ Homer

There was no question that Homer had been Annie's favorite horse. The bright chestnut gelding had left a racing career on the Quarter Horse circuit before changing careers to become her trail horse of choice.

Annie Dyson was a busy pediatrician. She also spent long hours working at The Dyson Foundation, a charitable organization. Annie had always said that Homer was what kept her sane. He was her therapy: when she got overwhelmed and couldn't take things anymore, the best cure was always a trail ride on Homer. After that, the world was all right once again.

Then Annie became very ill, and died. Sara, her barn manager, was left with the difficult task of selling or placing the horses in suitable homes. For some horses, it was easy. Who wouldn't want the world famous show hunter "The Wizard" in their barn? Wizard was gorgeous, had been Horse of the Year in the Working Hunter Division, and to boot was a major personality. Nobody could come in the barn without first paying homage to him. If you were naive enough to walk by, Wiz would bang on the door hard enough to stop you in your tracks. As soon as you retraced your steps, shame-facedly, to his stall, oohed and ahhed over him, and fed him his favorite butterscotch candies, he settled down.

Libby, the breathtaking chestnut mare who moved like Ginger Rogers (and knew it), made it easy. She chose her new owner. "Nope," she said, "not this one," as she tossed a perfectly suitable candidate into the forgiving rubber footing of the in-door..."Ah, this one is it, she is aware that I am a princess. She is the one."

Homer's virtues were not so apparent. He had not been

champion at Devon, nor did he possess the gorgeous movement of most of his stablemates. He was cute, with his broad white face, stocky body and two hind socks. Foaled in 1983, his racing name was Kitatip. His big haunches, wide back and thick neck were typical of the breed. But Quarter Horses are well known for their easy temperaments and Homer didn't quite fit the bill.

"Quirky" is the word most people would use to describe him. He was allergic to mounting blocks, perfectly aware that they often served as hiding places for horse eating prehistoric animals. If you got on him "cold" he would buck, and he proudly kept notches on his feed bucket for the number of riders he'd sent flying. In order for Annie to ride him, Sara would first lunge Homer for a short period. Then, once Annie was on, Sara would walk alongside him and tighten his girth a little bit. A short breather, then she would gingerly tighten it some more and Annie would be off to the trails.

Another one of Homer's quirks was that he was difficult to catch. To bring him in Sara would first have to catch all the other horses in the paddock. Only then would Homer consent to capture. His halter was a permanent fixture on his head, for once it came off you had a better chance of being abducted by aliens than catching Homer.

He could be a bit hot, so someone without experience was out of the question. Yet he was 18 and had an arthritic knee which rendered him less than sound, so an advanced rider probably wouldn't want him. He was not allowed to jump for fear that it would aggravate the knee. He was small, right around 16 hands. He had too many issues to be a child's mount and yet was too small for many adults. The cons seemed to outweigh the pros.

Placing him was a challenge, but Sara was determined to find him a good home. Annie and Sara had been very close. Sara had managed her barn for years. When Sara got married, Annie loaned her a beautiful house the Dysons owned on a ridge top affording spectacular views of the surrounding area as a place for the reception. Just before Annie died, Sara led the horses to Annie's bedroom window so she could say her good-byes to them.

So Sara took her task of placing the horses very seriously. It was particularly important to Sara to see that Homer was happy, because she was well aware of the place he held in Annie's heart. Annie had given Homer a good life, and Homer had repaid it with dividends. He was there for Annie when she went through an extremely painful divorce; he was always there to see her through whatever life could dish out. Annie needed Homer, and Homer needed to be needed.

Sara was excited when she found a home for Homer, one that seemed a good fit. He would be a hunt horse for Donna, the hunt master's wife. Donna was in her 60's and didn't want to jump. She only wanted to hilltop, trailing along behind the field. Homer took to it beautifully. He loved galloping out in the fields. And he was just around the corner from his former home, so Sara could check on him in his paddock on her way to work each morning.

Things went well at first. Homer got strong and fit. He appeared to be content in his new life, and even went south with his owners for the winter. Sara wished she'd managed that perk for herself! When they returned, he continued his work in the hunt field. Homer at 19 was getting more work than he'd ever gotten in his life, and thriving on it. His soundness issues disappeared and he became increasingly fit.

Too fit, unfortunately. He became too much horse for Donna, who became a little unnerved about riding him. He'd had a wonderful home for a year, but now he needed something else.

Sara was surprised. She thought that she'd found a good place for Homer. Yet, Sara sensed that something was missing. Homer was needed somewhere else, and that was why it hadn't worked. Homer had been so special to Annie, so important in her life. His present home was not one where Homer felt important. Homer knew his role and he relished it, wanting to be part of something larger in the scheme of things. Now he was ready to move on.

Sara started making phone calls again.

One of the calls Sara made was to Alice Fisher, who had been a good friend of Annie's and had been devastated by her death. When Annie was alive, Alice would come over and go trail riding with her. The two had been friends for years, dating back to their school days together at Bennett College. Alice would ride Henry, one of the Dyson girl's horses, and Annie would ride Homer.

Alice had helped Sara in her search to find homes for the horses. Initially, Sara had been too concerned about Homer's bucking to recommend him as a horse for Alice. Yet the idea of Alice getting one of Annie's horses appealed to her. Alice didn't have it easy. Bringing up two children alone was challenging and buying a horse wasn't in the single mom's budget.

Alice was lucky to have a brother, Ben, whom she was very close to. Although she had two other brothers, she and Ben shared a special bond. He was a great support for her.

But a horse in the family would be a nice addition.

Sara called Alice and let her know that once again she needed to find a place for Homer. Alice pitched in immediately, organizing a field trip with a friend to go and try him.

Alice was going to watch her friend ride Homer so she could see him go, then get on herself.

That changed when they arrived. Alice was the first one to get on Homer. She mounted, tightened his girth, and asked him to move forward. He didn't.

Glancing at Dick, Donna's husband, Alice asked, "What do I do?"

Dick, a horseman from way back, said "Well, kick him forward." His tone was clearly exasperated, as if to say "What do you think, dummy?"

Alice, a tad embarrassed, squeezed him forward. Homer responded with a cow kick. After the unpromising start, Alice headed into the ring, where she flatted a little bit and then asked Homer to jump a small fence. He refused, nearly dumping her in the dirt.

She heard Donna say "We're not to jump him Alice, Sara says we're not to jump him."

She thought, "Well that will change." And Homer went home with Alice.

Ben was thrilled when she got Homer. It pleased him so much that he threw a big parry for Homer, a party to welcome the horse to his new home and new life. Ben bought Alice a grooming box for her new horse filled with all kinds of supplies. Alice wasn't surprised. Ben was always her biggest supporter.

Sara liked to check up on her charges to see how things were going, and so, after a week, she called Alice. She got a glowing report. Homer adjusted beautifully and Alice just loved him! She'd turned him out in a large field with lots of trees, his summer home. Homer had spent a good part of his life in the posh surroundings of Annie's Shinto Farm. Alice told him, "Homer, I know you've been living at the Hilton, but this is the Days Inn, and it's the best I can do."

He dealt just fine, thriving out in the field with a buddy.

Sara checked again the second week, and then the third week. Things continued to go well. Homer was even getting easy to catch! Sara left for a well earned vacation, feeling relieved. It was August, 2001.

Sara returned home on September 10th, and promptly gave Alice a call. Things just kept getting better. Alice and Homer were jumping now. And Alice's four year old niece was helping with the grooming duties. She would squat next to Homer, brush his legs and paint his feet. She would even just slide under his belly to change sides! Homer, understanding his new role of babysitter, wouldn't move a muscle.

But, after that, Sara's phone calls were no longer returned. Starting to feel a bit uneasy, Sara tried many times. She got no response.

Then a letter arrived in the mail, a letter from Alice. "I really do apologize for my silence," Alice told her, "I couldn't talk to anyone."

Then the words started to sound familiar, words that Sara had so often heard from Annie. "I'm so grateful for Homer. I've been riding every day; he's been my therapy, my sanity. I would have gone crazy without him. We ride together through the country, and I sort out my feelings, and cry. The world isn't so bad when I'm on Homer.

You see, Sara, my brother Ben was last seen on the 44th floor of the World Trade Center on Tuesday, September 11th."

# ⤳ Blackie

**I**f there is one thing five year old girls know, it's how to get what they want. And Doreen wanted Blackie. He was a bag of bones, bound for the slaughterhouse, definitely not the kind of horse you picture your daughter on. Her parents tried to talk her out of it. They pointed out other, more suitable prospects: fat, slick horses any kid would be proud to call their own. They would have been happy to pay more than the asking price of $175 for Blackie in order to get their daughter a decent horse. Nope. With a child's instinct for the right thing, Doreen stubbornly held her ground. Blackie had come up and nuzzled her, choosing *her*, which was how it was supposed to be. "That's the one I want," she said again. And that was that.

Blackie was five, too, a Quarter Horse/Morgan cross that had definitely been in the wrong hands. In Doreen's care, he thrived. He grew fat and shiny and he never forgot who had changed his fate.

With no formal training to help them, Doreen and Blackie trained each other. Starting with a little bit of groundwork, in no time Doreen was on his back, working him with her voice. They did flatwork, progressing from simple walk, trot, canter, to barrels, trail riding and then jumping. He was so easy, eager to do whatever was asked of him. Even if Doreen didn't know how to ask, Blackie understood. Out on trail, logs would get in the way and Blackie would leap over them effortlessly. So the two started working on jumping in the ring. But Doreen preferred barrels. That was her favorite.

Some guidance was available from 4-H. The club would put on clinics and hold a camp. Lasting three days, the camp featured trainers in all disciplines. Pleasure classes were featured, and Doreen also learned a lot on horse care. The 4-H club didn't aim to produce just riders, but horsemen and women instead. Doreen learned to give public presentations on various horse topics as well as how to compete in shows.

Blackie could do anything and do it well. After only a year together, when Doreen and Blackie were six, they started competing. They showed in English and Western Pleasure, barrels, jumping, and even driving. Blackie didn't just excel in shows, he was also a true pleasure horse. Doreen could let anyone ride him and be confident that they would be safe on his back. In the warmer months he pulled a cart. In winter, he pulled a sled. Doreen could even get on him with no tack, not even a halter or a lead rope, and Blackie would do whatever she wanted. The pair rode in parades, where Blackie would bow to the judges. When they rode in a parade representing their 4-H group, they would wear the 4-H colors, with matching shirts, saddle pads and skid boots. Sometimes Doreen would stand in the saddle, waving the flag. At the Bicentennial parade in 1976, Blackie pulled the mayor of New York in his cart, a cart which had been built by Doreen and her father and painted red, white, and blue for the occasion.

As Blackie and Doreen grew up together, Blackie took an even more important place in her life. He became the babysitter for her two kids, Dennis and Chrissie. Just as the 15.1 hand gelding had been Doreen's first horse, he became her kids' first horse. Blackie's nickname had become "The King Man." Soon the plaques and trophies and belt buckles that line Doreen's home included ones won by her son and daughter.

Blackie's last show was at The Southern Dutchess Horseman's Association in Stormville, New York. A retirement ceremony was held for the champion whose reign had spanned generations. Dolled up in a red breastplate and red reins, Blackie galloped around the arena that he had owned for so long for one last time. On his back was Chrissie, only four years old, carrying the American flag.

At 36, Blackie colicked severely. The vets diagnosed a

twisted colon. They felt at his age he could survive the surgery, but wouldn't make it through the recovery. Doreen wanted badly to have the surgery done, but knew it would not be fair to her horse. She made the excruciating decision to have him put down. Blackie was given a fatal injection, but he wouldn't go out. So Doreen took his head and put it in her lap. He then closed his eyes and faded to horse heaven. He was waiting for Doreen to say "It's okay Blackie, you can go now."

Blackie is buried at her farm. The engraving on his tombstone is from a photo of Blackie running barrels with Dennis astride. In a local publication called *The Horseman's Directory*, Annie Secor eulogizes him:

*Just how do you earn the title "The King Man?" First you come with a smooth black coat and big, kind but mischievous brown eyes and you adopt a little "whirlwind with pigtails" tied with red ribbon and a big smile and take her to Championships in every division in every show in the area! You must have the best ground covering extended trot for Pleasure Shows and the best record in the "Carry The Mail" event in Gymkhanas! This has to be done without use of a crop, whip, spurs, or other speed-inducing aids. After all that, you must also have the same results for the children and friends of that "whirlwind with pigtails" during the next 10 or so years! Most importantly you must have a set of shoes that most horses wouldn't attempt to fill and a kingdom of friends that miss you a lot. That's how you get to be "The King Man!"*

# ⤚ᷓ Cosmo

He was just taking up space in a field when Pavel Blaho spotted him. Pavel knew who the horse was. He was big and beautiful, nearly 18 hands, a chestnut with white down the middle of his face. Pavel bought him.

The horse had been a top notch athlete, competing at the highest levels of the show world, but he was clearly not a ride for most people. In fact, someone came to try him, a top level rider who was looking for a horse for the Pan American Games. The man left without the horse: he couldn't ride him.

The horse, called Cosmo, attacked the jumps, going through them, running sideways at them. About five strides before a jump, he would lunge at them and take over, out of control.

But he was talented. And scopey. He definitely had the athletic ability and the speed to win in the big divisions. If anyone was capable of riding him, he was a bargain.

Michelle Clopp was an amateur rider showing in the jumpers. She had grown up riding strong, opinionated horses. Pavel gave her a call. "You might want to take a look at this horse."

Cosmo was difficult, extremely so, but Michelle hit it off with him.

Michelle needed a horse to show in the bigger jumper divisions, but couldn't afford what one would normally cost. Cosmo was athletic and affordable. She bought him.

Initially, Michelle said, "He was a machine. He would just come out of the stall, stand on the cross-ties and go to work. He didn't know what a carrot was."

Cosmo had, as Buck Brannaman* puts it, "gone somewhere else in his mind." When horses are in very stressful situations, they sometimes can't deal with it. So, to survive, they go somewhere else mentally. These horses become very aloof, like Cosmo.

Cosmo didn't seem to have a heart, he didn't care about anything, and he was so out of control that Michelle rarely even cantered him at home. They would just walk and trot, and go out on a lot of trail rides. The trail rides were good for keeping Cosmo fit, but to Cosmo they were terrifying experiences. The wind could blow a leaf or some other treacherous object in his path; a bird might fly overhead. He hated anything above his head: on a trail ride he never knew what might be up there.

Thunder and lightning would make him quiver in his stall, and snow could surely swallow him alive.

Yet in the ring Cosmo was fearless. The wind could snap flags around, fences could blow over and crash, it didn't matter. He would jump anything, no matter how big, or how wide, or how scary the course designers made it. Nothing stopped him; he would just go.

At the first show they went to, Cosmo broke his martingale and noseband. He ran at the jumps, lunging and plunging. There was no such thing as picking a distance. Cosmo was in control.

After that, Michelle rode him in two martingales and a rope noseband.

People watching Michelle ride Cosmo in the warm-up area would be shocked. "Are you going to let her go into the ring on that horse?" they would ask Sandy, Michelle's mother. "He's so crazy, he's dangerous!"

But he was competitive, and fast, so fast that he could win a speed class even with a rail down.

Despite his wild behavior, Sandy trusted Cosmo. She told people that, once he was in the ring, the horse was fine. "He knows his job." She knew that he would always jump. Whether it was the middle of the fence, or a standard, one couldn't be sure, but he would always go, and he could jump anything.

No bit worked on Cosmo. He could run through anything. That was, until Pavel went to a garage sale while he was in Europe. He found a bit there that seemed appropriate for Cosmo. He brought it home and handed it to Michelle. "Here," he said, "try this, this might work."

The bit did work. At least it was an improvement. It had a curb chain on it, and as long as the chain stayed attached, Michelle had some measure of control. But once he got that chain off, as Cosmo sometimes did, all bets were off. Sometimes Michelle would be in the middle of a class, and she would just have to quit, and leave the ring.

Michelle tried using boots, or polos, on Cosmo to protect his legs. That idea was quickly abandoned. Cosmo realized that now, if he hit the jumps, he didn't feel anything. This was all right, he thought. I can just take these poles with me. The polos came off.

At home, Cosmo hated to be groomed. Shows, however, were an entirely different story. Grooming had its place here. Cosmo knew he had to look his best for the show. He was so well behaved about it at a competition that he would pick his feet up and hold them carefully so Michelle could put caulks in.

Although Michelle and Cosmo began their show career in the adult amateur jumper division, they moved up quickly, graduating to the Amateur-Owner division. Cosmo was so scopey he could leave a stride out and never miss it. He always won enough prize money to pay his own way, and he and Michelle earned ribbons at top shows such as the Vermont Summer Festival and the Hampton Classic.

Along the way, Cosmo found his heart. Here, in Michelle, was a person he could trust, a person who cared about him not just as an athlete but as a friend.

Soon Cosmo became as addicted to shows as many exhibitors are. He would see the trunks being readied for loading and if he wasn't led to the van, he would buck in his stall. You didn't need to load him, he loaded himself. In fact, you better get out of his way or he might run over you in his hurry to get aboard.

The horse who once stuck his nose up at a carrot now ate just about anything. He loved Chinese food and seafood salad, and was known to steal apple pie if it was anywhere in the vicinity. Once, when a carrot cake meant for an employee's birthday was being carried down the aisle, he stuck his head out of his stall and sank his nose right into the middle of it.

Mints were his favorite. He loved to suck on them, and would practically go into a trance as they dissolved in his mouth.

When Michelle showed, Sandy came along. They were a mother-daughter travel team. Michelle worked in the horse show office at the Vermont shows to help support herself, so while she worked, Sandy would groom and tack Cosmo. Then Michelle would ride, and when she was finished, Sandy would take Cosmo back to cool him, while Michelle returned to work.

Sandy and Cosmo became a familiar sight on the showgrounds. Sandy would drive a four wheeler and Cosmo would tag happily along in her wake as they went in search of the best tasting grass.

Because of Michelle's work in the office, they would often be the last to leave a show. Michelle would come back to the tent, close up the ends and turn Cosmo loose inside. Then it was time to relax with some cocktails. Michelle and Sandy would have theirs, and Cosmo would have one, too.

Even after Cosmo was retired from showing, he still had to go to the shows. He quickly taught Michelle not to leave him behind. He got sick. In fact the first time Michelle left him he got so sick he nearly died. The vet told Michelle not to expect him to survive.

After that, Cosmo went along.

Cosmo came to Michelle a machine. He gave to her his athletic ability and competitive spirit. She gave him her gift of acceptance, not trying to "fix" him but letting him be himself. With love and acceptance, the horse who had "gone away" came back.

Buck Brannaman is a noted horse trainer who conducts

clinics throughout the country. The main character in "The Horse Whisperer" was largely based on him.

# ⌁ GRANDMA

Sugar was the kind of mare that took you by surprise. You could watch her all day, all night, run yourself ragged in trips out to the barn to see if the foal was on its way. But the second you let down your vigilance, got distracted by something else, boom, there was a foal.

And there was one now, out there in the snow. Kathy hadn't even seen it. Her guest had. She commented on the foal and Kathy said no, there was no foal. But there was. And the foal and its mom stood there in the snow in a little depression in the side of the hill.

Sugar, the foal's mother, was turned out with Dutchess, her own mother. The two chocolate brown Morgan mares often went out together. But today, it was clear that Dutchess knew she had become a grandmother, and that she had a role to play. She was circling mother and daughter, keeping all the other horses at bay.

The rest of the herd stood on top of the ridge, curious, but not daring to come near Dutchess. There was no question about her message. No one was to approach the newborn foal.

Kathy and her friend grabbed a halter and shank and headed for the field to bring in Sugar and her new baby. As they approached they could see Dutchess, circling, circling. Always keeping an eye on the other horses.

They walked into the pasture and Dutchess eyeballed them, but she didn't try to stop them. Soon they were in her protective circle as they approached. Was Kathy mistaken or did Sugar have a smirk on her face? She sure looked pleased with herself that she had once again outwitted the foal watchers.

She did allow herself to be caught and led towards the barn, her baby glued to her side.

Dutchess knew her job was not yet done. She kept circling about 50 feet from mother and baby, Kathy and friend. The other horses didn't move, kept in line by Dutchess's obvious orders.

Soon they were at the gate. Kathy opened it and Sugar and the baby slipped through. Dutchess stopped.

The door closed and was latched behind them. And suddenly Dutchess whinnied loudly. The other horses unfroze and once again went about their business, moving around the field.

The all clear had been sounded. Dutchess's daughter and newborn grandbaby were safely out of harm's way. All was right with the world again.

# ◦ SUNDANCE

It wasn't love at first sight, but there was interest. As a boy in kindergarten, Tyler used to drive by her every day on the school bus. Everyone on the bus noticed her; they all liked to gaze out the windows at her as they drove by.

She was different and she *was* pretty. Tyler thought she was kind of neat.

It was years later when Tyler, now in high school, became reacquainted with her.

Tyler had gotten a job at a barn near his home. Tyler was much like his mom, a real animal person. He was fascinated by wildlife, and very knowledgeable about birds. He spent more time with his animals than he did with people, so it was no surprise to anyone when he decided to take a job working with horses.

One day, a new horse arrived at the barn. It was the strawberry roan he had watched for years from the school bus. What Tyler didn't know was that she hadn't been treated too well. She and the two horses she'd lived with had been in a run-in shed that was two feet deep in manure. They were expected to survive on the sparse grass available to them in a small field. She was obviously the head mare, because she had fared better than the others. But the old horse that had lived with her was skinny, with ribs and hips showing plainly.

Sundance, as she came to be called, was turned out in a big field uphill from the barn. The barn manager thought the grass up there would help fatten her up. But it was a big field, and Sundance quickly proved to have a mind of her own. She wouldn't be caught. All the other horses in the barn had been wormed and had their shots; Sundance wouldn't cooperate.

Carol, the owner of the barn, became very frustrated as she tried over and over again. The horse wouldn't come near her, not even for grain.

Finally Tyler volunteered. Carol found it amusing. "You'll never catch her," she said.

Grabbing a halter and lead shank, Tyler walked out the back of the barn. He walked around the lower pasture, up the hill to the big flat field on top of the ridge, and continued through to the paddock in the back. It was a long walk.

Going into the last paddock, he saw the strawberry roan grazing. He walked up to her expecting her to flee. She didn't. He walked right up and placed the halter on her head. The mare stood patiently.

"I must have the wrong horse," Tyler thought. It couldn't be this easy. But he was sure she was the one. After all, he had watched her for all those years.

When he returned, Carol was amazed. "How did you catch her?" she asked.

"She came right up to me." Tyler said. Carol was pleased that she was caught, but jealous that it had been Tyler who caught her.

Tyler put the mare in a stall and took her halter off. Sliding the door behind him, he went back to work. Minutes later he heard loud bangs and crashes. It was Sundance. Unused to being in a stall, she was panicking. Bucking in the stall, kicking the walls, she was frantically trying to escape. She even managed to get her foot caught in a feed bucket.

In short order Carol decided she couldn't put up with the racket and ordered her out of the barn. The mare was crazy, she said. Tyler put her back in the field, where she stayed for a while, once again left to be wild. Soon Carol decided it was time to be rid of her, swayed both by her performance in the barn and by her disloyalty to Carol in letting Tyler catch her.

But Tyler had been thinking. He had never owned a horse before, never even ridden one. Yet this crazy mare had come to him.

Maybe she was supposed to be his. Besides, it would be sort of cool to own a wild horse.

He worked for four months without pay to earn the horse.

Then he rode her. A rank beginner on a horse that hadn't been ridden for 11 years.

It wasn't a pretty sight. Sundance refused to go forward, spinning and running backwards so fast she stepped on her own tail, yanking her hind end almost out from under her. But Tyler stayed on her and kept urging her forward. He finally succeeded.

Perhaps a wild horse *wasn't* such a great idea. Tyler hired a trainer to give the horse a good start under saddle. Meanwhile, he worked with her on the ground. She improved. Stalls no longer were terrifying places, and Tyler was soon able to easily groom and work around Sundance. She became more and more attached to him and soon they were going for long trail rides together.

Sundance was still high strung, but she was good for Tyler. She could, like all the creatures and people around him, feel his innate love for animals.

Sundance would prance when she walked, and her trot was always long and low and big, an eye catching gait.

Things changed at the barn. It was no longer an enjoyable place to be, so Tyler brought Sundance home. There were no horses, but there was a fenced in yard with ducks, and chickens and a big pig named Darla. Sundance thought that was fine and soon she and Darla were best buddies.

It's been three years since Tyler bought his "wild" horse, and the bond between them has produced a marked change in the mare. Now a family pet, and everyone's riding horse, Sundance loves life on the farm. She lies flat out in the sun, catching her rays. Tyler's sister, mother, and cousins all take her out on trail rides.

The day that Tyler climbed the hill to the big pasture on the ridge behind the barn, he thought he was going out to catch a horse.

Little did he realize that she was catching him.

# ⟶ TRACKING

Your dog is missing, your wife is frantic, and you're hundreds of miles away, planning to spend some time with your two sons. What do you do?

Well, the first thing you do is cancel plans with the kids (who, animal lovers themselves, are completely understanding). Then you head home, as fast as you can reasonably drive.

Once you're home, you and your wife head out on foot, looking for the missing Jack Russell terrier named Oreo. You live in an area not all that heavily populated with humans, an area that has quite a well deserved reputation for its coyote population. So the search becomes all the more pressing.

Oreo had escaped the previous night when Ron Moloff's wife, Liz, was walking him. Actually she had been walking both Oreo and Cody, their Catahaula Leopard Hound, when Cody ran into Liz, causing her to drop Oreo's leash. Liz had been enjoying the 1500 acres adjoining the Moloff's property when both Cody and Oreo disappeared into the wilderness.

Cody reappeared later that night, minus Oreo. And Oreo, Liz knew, was dragging a long leash with its retractable handle bouncing behind. It was not a good accessory for a foray into the woods.

When Ron reached home, Oreo had been missing close to 24 hours. It was pouring as Ron and Liz donned their rain gear and ventured out in search of her. They were both worried and depressed, neither holding much hope of finding the little dog.

Ron tried to hide his anxiety, attempting to be strong for his wife's benefit. For two hours they searched, calling for Oreo.

Cody came along, and Ron asked him to "Go find Oreo." Just like in the movies. Only, Ron said, Cody didn't "rush off to play hero."

They returned home without Oreo. Both of them were tired and miserable, and rapidly losing any hope.

Toward evening, Ron noticed their farm manager's car in the driveway. Walking into the barn he stopped Concho, who had just started to feed the horses, and explained the situation to him.

It was almost six p.m., and it would be getting dark soon.

"I'll go out again on one of the horses in the morning and resume the search. I'm exhausted," Ron told Concho.

Concho looked at him. He was more concerned with Oreo's life than Ron's fatigue. "There are coyotes out there," he reminded Ron. And it had already been almost 36 hours since the dog disappeared.

Ron conceded the point. No matter how exhausted he was, he had to go out again. He told Concho not to say anything to Liz about the coyotes, and asked him to help saddle up Brisa. Brisa is Ron's gorgeous chestnut Paso Fino filly, a filly with whom Ron placed third in the National Championships. Ron had spent months fussing over Brisa's mother before she was born, and then delivered the filly himself. He spent years training her, developing a closer bond with her than with almost any other horse he'd ever had.

Ron put on a rain slicker, mounted Brisa, and set off once again with Cody on his flank. Deeper and deeper into the woods they went, but Ron was feeling that it was probably a futile mission. How could Oreo possibly have survived with all the coyotes? And if she had, someone had probably found her and decided to keep her. Yet he had to try, for Oreo's sake, and to ease his wife's suffering.

Eventually Ron had to call it quits for the evening. Darkness was rapidly setting in, and the rain continued to obscure his vision. Ron decided to take a different route home, one that he didn't often take. For a brief stretch, Ron and Brisa emerged out of the woods into a clear area along the power line. Then they were back in the woods as Ron called Oreo's name for one last time. There was a sharp screech and two crows flew out of the trees.

What was it? Was it the crows, or had they heard something else? Ron wasn't sure where the noise had come from. They rode toward the direction of the birds, and again Ron called Oreo's name. Again, there was a noise, although it was weaker this time. Cody had disappeared, and Brisa suddenly of her own accord, reversed direction. Did she know something Ron didn't know? She certainly seemed to know where she was going.

Ron called Oreo once again

This time his call was answered by a nearly hysterical scream. Riding toward the noise, Ron feared they would come upon a coyote pack attacking poor Oreo. As they crossed through an opening in a stone wall, the cries became frantic. Ahead, Ron could see Cody sitting next to a tree.

And there she was. Little Oreo with her leash wrapped around the tree, next to Cody. She was alive!

Ron got off Brisa, tied her lightly to a tree, ran to his muddy dog and hugged her. Oreo kept yelping, licking his face joyfully. Brisa stood quietly, letting Ron and Oreo enjoy their reunion.

When they were almost home, Ron could see Liz ahead. She was trying to distract herself by weeding one of the flowerbeds.

"Come take a picture," he called.

"What a jerk!" thought Liz. My little angel Oreo is missing and all my husband cares about is getting a photo taken of him with his horse. But when she came up the hill and saw the little terrier, she burst into tears. Ron joined her, crying in excitement and exhaustion.

Oreo was awash in hugs and kisses.

Brisa just stood quietly by. She was no prima donna. The star of the show world could track, too!

# ⤳ Ben

by Linda Eder

Every horse lover who is lucky enough to be in a position to own horses knows that horses are like potato chips. You can't have just one. I have owned 12 horses over the course of my life so far. I currently own three and with any luck I am sure that the numbers will continue to grow over the next years. I have owned everything from expensively bred to grade and my favorite to this day is a dark chocolate brown Quarter Horse named Ben. He is small, only fifteen hands. Yet even at 21 years young he remains pound for pound the best horse I have ever owned.

Ben's mother Quarter Bar Dee was the first horse I purchased as an adult. She was the same dark seal brown and well bred. I bought her already in foal and my excitement grew along with her belly. Bad luck would have it that I was out of town driving 1200 miles back home when (Barbie) decided to foal. I missed the birth by two hours, but that was the last thing I missed in the early life of Mercedes Benz. I imprinted this colt long before I knew what that term meant. We were buddies. One of the things I remember most from our early days was the game of tag. I would chase the three month old and then he would turn around and chase me. It was the beginning of a relationship that has continued to this day and allowed me to learn the mind and colorful personality of this wonderful animal.

As Ben grew to maturity it became clear that the man who had planned the breeding knew a thing or two about horses. Ben was big in all the right places and refined where you wanted refinement. He stood in the way that old timers called "legs at all four corners." His angles were all correct and aside from the fact that part of his mane wanted to hang on the wrong side he was perfect. It's a common practice to judge a horse's character by the size and shape of the eye. I'm not sure that I believe that completely, but if it's true then Ben's eyes proved that. They were large and beautiful and slightly lighter than the average making them a warm gold color. He had no white except for a beautiful star and strip that ran down the center of his face.

I had never trained a horse myself, but when the time came Ben made my job easy. He never bucked or behaved badly and he learned quickly. I'm convinced that he would have made a good trick horse because of his brain and his desire for human companionship.

I have always turned my horses out together in a large pasture free to form their own herd. Horses have come and gone, but no matter what the mix or size, Ben is always the leader. He is two hands shorter than some of my current horses, but he doesn't know it. He takes his job very seriously and I should have him on the payroll. Even when work makes my riding sporadic, he keeps everyone in shape. Every evening like clockwork he rounds them all up for an hour of exercise. He whips his little herd into a frenzy of running, bucking and playing that is a joy to watch.

Ben comes from racing bloodlines and true to his Quarter Horse reputation he can run like the wind for a quarter mile. I will never forget the first time I let out his engine. His little ears went back and like an expensive sports car he got suddenly low over the road and took off. The wind howled in my ears and tears ran out of the corners of my eyes. When we stopped his ears came up and he grew three inches. He had enjoyed it as much as I had and from then on whenever we came to a safe stretch of road or trail he would wait for me to give the signal.

Aside from the occasional feeling fresh "crow hop" Ben has never reared, run away, or bucked in disobedience. He did however throw me off by accident. We were riding along the edge of my pasture and the rest of the herd came to the fence to say hello. As we started to move on again the herd took off in a cloud of good spirits, bucking and snorting and passing copious amounts of gas the way horses seem to do when ever they torque their midsections. Well, Ben forgot that he was not part of the herd at that moment and threw some big bucks of his own. Totally unprepared I went from sitting in the saddle to flying straight up into the air and landing upright on my knees in the deep hay field. Ben stood a few feet to my left and turned his head looking down at me as if to say, "How did you get there?" He seemed as surprised as I was. I had a good laugh all the way back to the barn.

Through our early years together Ben tolerated my forays into a variety of disciplines: reining, barrels, jumping, dressage, but our partnership and friendship has really been created on the many, many miles of trails we have wandered. Anyone who rides can attest to the value of a horse you feel safe on. Ben has always been that horse for me. Though he has always been too smart and sensitive to comfortably put a beginner on he is a dream trail horse because he is brave and trusting and whenever anything would happen that was truly startling to both of us his only reaction would be to drop straight down under me a few inches while he braced himself to look. In all our years of riding the trails we only faced one scary moment and his trusting brave nature got him through it.

The hunt for new terrain is part of trail riding and I remember the day when my carelessness got us into trouble. We set out on a warm summer day through woods and over fields around my farm in Minnesota. I was in the mood for a long ride and Ben had his ears up and was ready to go. Eventually we were riding through a field that I didn't know. The grass was over Ben's knees, but the ground was firm. Halfway through the field we came to a narrow irrigation ditch that ran the length of it. There was no way to go around, but because it was only a few feet across I knew we could easily jump it. Ben had no fear of water so we backed up a bit and over we went. What I didn't know was that although the field looked the same on the other side it was anything but. The minute we landed I knew we were in trouble. Ben heaved a few paces forward and then got bogged down in thick mud and fell over onto his side, buried in the high grass. I stood beside him feeling my own feet slowly sinking down into what felt like quicksand. The grass was up to my chin. Ben tried to get up and flailed a bit before falling back onto his side. I had a few moments of real panic. We were miles away from help and I was afraid for Ben. This is when the trusting nature of this horse saved the day. Had he panicked he could have caused himself real harm. Instead he calmed down when I said "Easy, Ben" and kept his gold colored eyes on mine the whole time. He lay there looking at me while I unhooked one rein and tied it onto the end of the other giving me a longer rope to put myself a safer distance from his front legs and at the same time giving him something to balance his weight against. He waited until I called and as I pulled to steady his head and neck he heaved himself forward one large stride and then waited when I said "whoa". He again fell sideways but he stayed calm as the water and mud pulled at him and he all but disappeared in the grass. I worked myself backwards until the rein was taut again and we repeated this. What felt like hours was probably twenty minutes but eventually we worked our way through the muck and grass until I felt solid ground under my feet. Through this whole ordeal my little horse never took his eyes off mine and seemed to understand that he needed to listen to me. He trusted me and that day in our young lives together cemented a relationship that continues to this day.

As I said I have other horses. I have the big fancy seventeen point two hand warmblood that floats like a cloud and turns heads. She also shies at the same mailbox every time, won't walk through an inch of water and occasionally misbehaves just "because." Whenever we take them all out for a trail ride and hit a "spooky patch" it's Ben who marches in the lead. He came as a gift in the belly of my first grown up horse and he will probably reign forever as pound for pound the best horse I have ever known. My buddy, Ben.

# ⤳ KEATON

He was never supposed to be a Grand Prix horse. She didn't know how to ride one.

Flashpoint (Keaton) was a mutt, the son of a broken down school horse who somehow managed a date with All the Gold. He was born with a club foot and a bad attitude. At two, he nearly died of colic and required surgery. Along the way he managed to accumulate bone chips in his ankles and knees.

He came with a lot of spots, his golden chestnut coloring splashed everywhere with white.

As a baby, he quickly let his opinions be known to whatever and whoever was around him. He didn't want to be caught, led, or otherwise messed with. As he grew, he only became more difficult. His halter had to be left on at all times, or you would never catch him. Walk in his stall and he would fly at you to take a bite. Then he would wheel and let you have it with the other end.

The paddock was even more of a challenge. He became so hard to approach that the only solution was to hop on a golf cart and go into the paddock in your armored vehicle.

Stacie Shepski was the trainer at the farm where Keaton lived. Stacie was young, a trainer with a lot of horse sense, but not a lot of experience behind her. The owner's daughter began Keaton's training and Stacie started riding him when he was almost three. As bad as he was in the barn, he was good to ride. He didn't try to buck or rear or do any stupid baby tricks.

He did, however, continue to be opinionated. He wanted to do things, but to do them his way. Stacie didn't try to change him; she just let him be himself.

One day, at three and a half, Keaton had his first experience with jumps. Everyone was wondering if, given his father (who is a leading sire of show hunters), he had any talent for jumping. Although he wasn't about to begin his over fences training yet, they all wanted to get an idea of what he could do.

It was a disaster. Keaton was horrible, probably one of the worse jumpers anyone had ever witnessed. He made no effort to pick up his legs, letting them dangle straight down from his chest.

It looked like a career in the hunter divisions would not be an option.

Stacie continued to train him and Keaton continued to let her know that his way was the only way.

Later, Keaton's over fences career actually began, it was a reality check. Jacking the fences up made no difference in the horse's style. He continued to jump just as poorly, leaving legs behind in all directions.

But he did jump higher.

And he was quick. His dam's Quarter Horse heritage gave him speed and agility.

Despite his extremely unorthodox style, Keaton was careful. He didn't feel any particular need to tuck his knees and round his back and look pretty, but he didn't want to hit the poles either. Stacie found that she needed to be very accurate. The horse didn't want to get himself in trouble, and he trusted that Stacie wouldn't put him to a bad spot.

By the time he was five, the unstylish jumper and untutored rider were showing in the modified jumpers, and doing well. People were talking. At the time, pintos were not often seen in the world of hunter/jumpers, and Stacie had no name as a rider. She came out of nowhere with no record. She was uneducated, riding off the seat of her pants. The horse was unbroke and Stacie was the first to admit it.

The team had "no right" to be doing so well. Yet they were.

And they were a team. Stacie babied Keaton, icing his legs, hand walking him, training him lightly. She never jumped him at home, and at a show three or four schooling jumps were all she needed before they headed into the ring. She did not clash with his opinions. They had a deal. She pointed him at a jump and he jumped it; in exchange she let him do it *his* way.

The team was doing so well in the modifieds, there was only one way to go. Up. To the next step: the Grand Prix.

In 1994 Stacie and Keaton were in their very first Grand Prix: for both of them. They came third.

The following week they were third again in the Grand Prix.

Again, people talked. Who was this girl? And a spotted horse? In the Grand Prix? *Never!*

It didn't stop them. Out of 11 Grand Prix entered, they placed in 10. Near the end of the season, Keaton and Stacie stood first in the standings for Rookie of the Year.

That lasted until Harrisburg.

Here, experience proved essential and Stacie and Keaton were way over their heads. The massive jumps and technical course proved their undoing and they finished with 12 faults.

The winner of that year's Rookie of the Year title was Elizabeth Solter. If you're going to lose, why not lose to the best?

Stacie moved on to a better job in New York. Keaton did well for a short time with a new rider, but soon lost his enthusiasm. His partner was gone. He didn't want to jump for anyone else. It was part mental, part physical, but it was clear. His success had been due to teamwork. A rider who, though uneducated, had the tact to know when to let the horse make decisions, and a horse who, despite many issues, wanted to give back to his rider.

The bond between the two was what made their success, which seemed impossible, work.

Keaton retired young. Stacie works with a topflight barn in New York. Neither will forget each other, and being part of a team that made dreams a reality.

# Rescues

# ⌁ IROQUOIS

Talk about a life changing event. Allene Simmons had no idea how dramatically her life would differ when she decided to add a couple of horses (just pets) to her backyard.

Wheaten Terriers, goats, and alpacas already played in the fields. But, the lively redhead thought, horses would be a nice addition.

Allene had read about rescue operations, people who took Thoroughbred racehorses and gave them a new start in life, often saving them from slaughter. She mentioned to her lawyer that she was interested in some horses. He just happened to know a woman, Suzanne Wagner, who ran a rescue operation named Equine Advocates.

Suzanne was not shy about rescuing horses: if it meant going right into a slaughterhouse, she would do so. And in a slaughterhouse is where she found Iroquois Hills and Lily on a scale where they were being weighed out for meat. Literally minutes from being slaughtered, the horses caught Suzanne's eye. It was a telling moment. She knew that they had to be saved.

Iroquois and Lily each needed to go to a "half-way" house before they could be turned over to Allene. Lily was heavily drugged and had to go straight. Iroquois, a sensitive soul who had been badly mistreated on the track, was angry and mean. He had to learn that there were humans out there who were trustworthy.

So the horses spent two months decompressing at Bright Future's Farm with Beverlee Dee and then were shipped to Ailene's home. She wasn't sure what to expect, but was eagerly awaiting her new pets.

Two dark bay horses walked off the van. Lily looked all right, but Iroquois, who had had to be weaned off of steroids (Beverlee says when he first arrived he looked more like a cutting horse than a Thoroughbred race horse), didn't have a lot of muscle tone. In fact he was a tad flabby.

The horses came with some impressive bloodlines. Lily was a granddaughter of Affirmed; Iroquois Hills was a grandson of Damascus and he had won two races, placed second in one, and third in another. What were these two sound and beautifully bred youngsters doing in a slaughterhouse?

Iroquois Hills had been saddled with a barn name of Fabio by his rescuers. Allene didn't think it fit. Iroquois was too macho to be stuck with such a name. His barn name became "Beau."

Allene was very careful with her new charges, spending a week just handling them, getting them accustomed to their surroundings. At first they were just big pets, which was all she wanted. Horses to groom, ride around the paddock, maybe do a trail ride here and there.

It didn't take long for that to change. Allene had been a top show rider, exhibiting champion Saddlebreds and roadsters (including three World Champions and five National Champions) at Madison Square Garden. She had trained with the legendary Helen Crabtree. She thought she had put that all behind her, the huge amounts of time, money, and effort involved in showing. Yet her competitive spirit kept nudging her. These horses could do more, much more, than be pets.

So she worked with them, using her old horsemanship skills to teach them flatwork. As a young child she had done some jumping and she remembered how much fun it was. Maybe the horses could learn to jump, too.

Before Allene adopted her horses, there were power lines scattered around her back yard. They were unsightly and a danger to the horses. Allene had a work crew come in and bury them. Although the lines were now underground, the heavy poles they had been attached to remained. A thought glimmered in Allene's head.

"What do you do with them?" she asked the workmen.

"Oh, we just get rid of them."

The workmen did not get rid of the poles. Instead they were bundled together and placed throughout the fields in small piles, making excellent jumps. They were the start of many jumps that now grace the property and were one of many changes the property underwent.

It was so much fun jumping Iroquois and Lily that soon Allene added to her collection. Patio furniture, picnic benches, boxes piled on top of one another all became subject to jumping horses.

The collection of horses grew, too. Allene was having such a good time with them that Beverlee asked her if she wanted another one. "What color is it?" the interior decorator in Allene asked.

"Red," said Bev.

That would add some color to the group, Allene thought.

Top Gun's Fly Free (Gunner) joined the others at the farm. Now Allene had three horses to jump.

While Allene's property was undergoing a transformation into a playground for hunters and jumpers, her wardrobe had yet to catch up. That was quickly remedied. Hunter/jumper riders require a very traditional and elegant look. Breeches, ratcatcher shirts, tall boots, and jackets all soon found a home in Allene's closet.

In her past Allene had confined herself to the rarefied world of the gaited horse. Now that she had Thoroughbreds, it was time to do what the Thoroughbreds did best. Running and jumping was what competitors did in hunter paces and hunter trials. So that's what they did. The more she did, the more Allene loved it. It was exhilarating.

To get the horses to the paces and trials, Allene hired a commercial shipper because she didn't have a trailer of her own. Not at first, anyways.

It didn't take too long for the cost of shipping the horses to begin to add up. It was inconvenient, too. She couldn't just pick up and go whenever she wanted to. Arrangements had to be made, schedules adjusted to. So Allene went out and bought her three "pets" a trailer.

A big day arrived when Allene purchased her first "official" jump, a pair of PVC standards and poles. She started jumping Beau over it, and raising it higher and higher. By the time she stopped, it was huge. Four feet. "This horse has some talent," she thought.

Winter was setting in and all Allene had for her horses was a paddock and run-in shed. There was no way she was about to let Beau, who had rapidly become her best friend, spend the winter in less than ideal conditions. So, Beau, Lily, and Gunner were sent to North Carolina for three months. The horses were turned out and fed. With no work and lots of food they got fat. And sassy.

When the horses returned to New York, they were not the quiet, cooperative mounts that had left Allene's in the fall. They remembered their racehorse heritage. They were fast and high.

Allene could barely control Beau any more. When her friend, Mary Dzenutis, stopped by one day to watch her ride, Mary gently suggested Allene could use some help. And she knew someone: Don Patterson.

Don came to see the horses. They were wild and not sure what they were doing. But there was one indisputable fact. They were highly talented. Lily seemed to have the makings of a show hunter, while Beau belonged in the jumper ring, with Gunner hot on his heels.

He couldn't help but be amused by Allene's luck. Her horses had been rescued from the slaughterhouse at the last minute, and yet they were top class horses. Not bad work for someone who chose them sight unseen.

He watched Allene and Beau and quickly assessed that neither one knew what they were supposed to do with the jumps. He suggested Allene get herself a quiet school horse that knew its job, so she could learn to jump. Meanwhile, Don would school Beau and teach the horse how to do his part.

Allene's reaction was immediate and not open to argument.

No way. She and Beau would learn together. End of story.

The first lesson lasted about an hour and a half. It consisted of trying to get Beau to trot over a rail on the ground without lunging, plunging, and running sideways.

Don knew this wasn't going to be easy. He also quickly discerned something crucial. Beau would never have made it to the show ring with most riders. Although quiet and easy going on the ground, in a show Beau was a bundle of sheer anxiety. He was not an easy ride and his combination of talent and anxiety could have proved disastrous under someone less understanding. Allene did not have much experience with jumpers. What she did have was the intuitive knowledge that this horse needed time and patience. And she had the love for the horse that let her give him what he needed.

The first few shows could politely be described as learning experiences. Beau would just race at the jumps, barely getting his feet out of the way in time.

At a small show in Massachusetts, Beau insisted on racing around the course like a maniac and flinging himself over the jumps in a heap just to get them over with.

Dripping wet, and white with foam, the horse needed a bath.

So Allene took him to the wash stall. It was tiled in white ceramic with stainless steel fixtures, very bright, very antiseptic. Reminiscent of…a slaughterhouse.

Beau took one look at it and planted his feet in the ground.

Beau's first encounter with a liverpool didn't go well either. At that same show in Massachusetts, Beau came around a sharp turn and found himself face to face with a liverpool (with no water in it). It surprised him and he tried to stop, instead sliding right into it. The thing skittered across the ground, making terrifying noises. It was months before anyone could convince Beau that most liverpools do *not* house monsters.

When Beau started to figure things out a bit and adjust to horse shows, Don decided he was ready for something a little more challenging. He and Allene took Beau to Old Salem Farm in North Salem, New York. There Beau had his first encounter with a water truck. It was bad enough Beau was expected to jump terrifying live things, now he had to face a sea monster spouting water at him. He flipped out, and went home for the day.

His next trip to Old Salem was far more successful. He came home with some good ribbons in Level 1 and Level 2 jumpers.

Allene was happy with the ribbons and how well Beau was going. But she was distracted. Old Salem has a large, beautifully landscaped Grand Prix field where several Olympic trials have taken place. Her eyes kept roving to that field. Wasn't that where she and Beau were supposed to be?

Meanwhile, at her home, the one paddock and run-in shed had proven to be insufficient quarters. Allene added more paddocks and had a barn built. A large field now sprouted all kinds of fences, from natural logs to gymnastic lines to huge oxers. Jumps now adorned just about every area of the property. A dressage ring was built in an adjacent corner. The property bears little resemblance to its "Pre-horse" days when Allene purchased it in 1997.

When Allene first adopted the horses, she owned two homes: a one bedroom apartment on Fifth Avenue in New York City, and the one in Dutchess County where she kept them. That, too, soon changed. After September 11th, Allene knew that she could no longer live in the city. Besides, she had the horses to consider. They needed a better life. She couldn't have them struggling through the cold winters of upstate New York.

The one bedroom apartment in New York City was soon sold and the money was used to purchase a horse farm in Florida. Now the horses had winter quarters.

As soon as the days began to get cool, Allene and Don packed up the horses and headed south to the new farm. Soon the Wellington (West Palm Beach) circuit was in full swing, and they started competing.

At Littlewood, Allene and Beau earned many good championships in Level 2, and Adult Amateur Jumper classes, and qualified for the Marshall and Sterling finals. Allene became more and more aware of Beau's scope, and of how much heart he has. When Allene, like all amateurs, makes a mistake, even a major mistake like burying him to a huge oxer, Beau doesn't stop. He just tries harder.

It wasn't just Allene's properties and lifestyle that totally changed as the horses became more and more prominent in her life. Allene's businesses, too, had to adapt. An interior designer and real estate developer, Allene now divides her time to follow the show circuit.

In the winter, she works in Florida. She spends four months (summer and early fall) at the farm in Clinton Corners, attending shows such as Old Salem and HITS Saugerties, and flying to Florida as needed to attend to her businesses.

With the success that Allene and Beau began to achieve, it was time to move up to more challenging classes. It was also time to find someone to coach her.

Don trains the horses, and keeps them fit and schooled for the ring. He and Gunner have been stars in their own right, taking the High Jumper Championship for the Littlewood Circuit last winter.

While Don is busy with the horses, Allene needed someone who could concentrate specifically on her riding, to be her coach. She chose Michael Mueller (who has coached Nona Garson). With Michael's help, she and Beau competed in the "Senior Amateur Division" (for riders over 45). The classes were huge, averaging 60 riders. Beau and Allene got some good ribbons.

When Allene's good friend Denise Monopoli decided to go to The Kentucky Classic Horse Show held at the Kentucky Horse Park, Allene decided to go along. She entered Beau in the Amateur-Owner Jumpers, which was supposed to be a Level 5/6. But when she looked at the ring the fences were tremendous, approaching a level 7.

Pablo Barrios (who had already won a Grand Prix there and was second and third in the other two) was helping Allene. He wasn't sure she was ready for the very large and technical course. Should he let her go? He consulted with Denise.

Denise's advice was "Just don't let her know what you're thinking." She figured that if Allene thought it was okay with Pablo, then Allene and Beau would manage to pull it off.

Admittedly, Allene was nervous. But she wanted to see if she and Beau could do it.

Things were going all right until they got to the mammoth triple combination. Allene didn't get Beau to the right spot. Most horses would have quit. Not Beau. He tried. He took some rails with him, but he got through the combination. Denise and Pablo, watching, thought the same thing, "That horse has heart!"

The show proved to be a major high for Allene, because she and Beau had taken on a huge challenge and, together, they had done it. Beau is, Allene says, "such a tryer. He doesn't know the word failure. Even when I miss badly he always keeps jumping, he takes care of me."

The once flabby five-year-old is now a fat and well rounded nine-year-old. He no longer needs steroids to make his chest massive and his rump strong and well muscled. His build makes him look substantial, far bigger than the 16 hands he actually measures.

And, while he takes care of Allene, she takes care of him. They still do hunter paces because "He's a Thoroughbred, and Thoroughbreds love to run."

Beau gets his vacation time, too. Allene hops on bareback and rides him on her beach. ("Who needs to go to the Hamptons?" she thought, and had a beach built on the pond in her backyard). Together they splash through the pond. Sometimes Allene relaxes on her lounge chair on the beach, while Beau rolls in the sand next to her.

Going away can be a problem for Allene. Beau gets too angry. Even if it's just for a few days, Allene comes home to the silent treatment and the angry face.

Allene can see the beach from the back windows of the house. Sometimes in the middle of the day she'll look out and see Beau with a buddy, hanging out in the shade of the big beach umbrella. As she looks at Beau, she thinks, "That's my best friend."

Allene and Beau finished off 2004 with a double clear at The National Horse Show, placing them sixth in the country in the adult amateur jumpers.

That marked their swan song in the division; they have now graduated to the "senior" amateur-owner jumpers...and to the grand prix field! This isn't just any grand prix field, it's the International Arena at the Winter Equestrian Festival.

They did need to find a new coach, as Michael decided not to go to Florida this year. With the new coach, Allene and Beau have been training beautifully, and Allene credits him with taking them to a whole new level.

Allene and Beau want to "get as good as we can" so that they can "see what we can do." In three years Beau has come from a last minute reprieve from the slaughterhouse to winning good ribbons in the toughest horse show circuits in the country. Allene has come from jumping boxes and lounge chairs to the Grand Prix Field.

Allene gave Beau a new life.

And when you let a horse into your life, you never know where you'll end up.

# MacGregor

He was old, skinny, and lame, decrepit as a matter of fact. But the chestnut Quarter Horse came right over to Michelle as she stood at the fence. That was all it took. She couldn't leave him behind.

He turned out to be the best school horse she's ever had.

MacGregor was one of three horses hanging out in a paddock. His two owners had told their new housekeeper to "just get rid of the horses." In fact, the owners wanted her to send them off to be used for experimental research.

That, she was not about to do. So she made some phone calls. One was to a woman who was a friend of Michelle Clopp. The friend knew that Michelle's mother, Sandy, worked with a therapeutic riding program, and she thought perhaps one or more of the horses could fit that program.

So Michelle and Sandy came to have a look. And when MacGregor came to the fence to look back at them, he found a new home.

Michelle was working in Vermont at the time, so she wasn't around her New York barn to spend time with the new horse. She gave the assignment to a ten-year-old kid, a student at the barn. MacGregor was to be her project: she was to clean up his long neglected coat, work with him and get the horse fit so that he would be ready for his new job as a school horse.

Michelle wasn't sure what to expect. She definitely wasn't expecting a star.

MacGregor turned out to be a trooper. Everyone who came

to MLC farm to learn to ride, learned on MacGregor. From the tiniest kid to the biggest adult MacGregor took care of them all. He would just keep going, sticking to the rail, giving the new riders a nice, perfectly even pace to learn to post, to learn their diagonals on. No one had to kick and push to keep MacGregor going, he just motored along.

MacGregor wasn't only the first horse people rode, he was the first one they showed. The same power steering and evenness of pace could make even a not so swift rider look like a winner. In pole classes, MacGregor reigned. Other horses might duck out or cut in; MacGregor marched right around, jumping down the middle, going into his corners, and being a perfect gentleman. By maintaining that even rhythm, MacGregor would basically find his own distances.

Riding MacGregor almost guaranteed a blue ribbon. But it wasn't just the ribbons the riders won on him. They won their confidence, too.

MacGregor could aptly be nicknamed Houdini, for he is quite an escape artist. No gate can keep him somewhere if he decides that somewhere else is more interesting. (He can always take it off its hinges if it proves too troublesome to undo the fastener.) And despite his advanced age of thirty something, MacGregor is not past jumping over a wheelbarrow in front of his stall if he decides he wants out.

One day someone told Sandy that MacGregor was in the office. "Sure he is," she thought. But he was. He had not only escaped his stall, he had made his way into the office where he was happily searching for treats.

At one point, MacGregor bowed a tendon. He was already an elderly horse, and Michelle and Sandy both feared it was the end of his career. But he came back sound. His work load was lightened, and made easier by no longer asking the old man to canter.

Instead of being sacrificed, MacGregor was rescued. By saving that one life, Michelle and Sandy have changed the lives of many. MacGregor has repaid their kindness a thousand times by introducing kids and adults to the joys of riding and the pleasure of a horse's company.

# ⌐⊷ JOURNEY

**W**here would you look for an award winning dressage horse? Would you go to Europe and shop in elite barns, barns that have Olympic champions on their roster of past sales? Or would you head to one of the big warmblood breeding farms in the U.S., ones that take up a quarter of the *Chronicle of the Horse's* breeding issue with their pages and pages of top stallions? Maybe you would start with a youngster, one that was a blank slate for you to write your own ticket to greatness on.

One horse you probably wouldn't consider would be one that you drove by on your way home, an unkempt horse with western gear, walking along on the pavement, going who knows where.

Penny Hawes remembers seeing Journey the first time. It was May, 1991. She had lived in Cornwall, Connecticut nearly all her life, and she knew just about every horse in the area. This horse wasn't local. He was about 16 hands, an attractive bay. The rider on his back looked young, probably in her early twenties. Penny was traveling along Route 4, a major artery in the area, and she wondered where the pair was going. From the tack and equipment, it looked like they were on a long haul. Penny thought to herself "That's a nice horse."

A few days later, she picked up a local paper, the *Torrington Register*. In it there was a photo of the same woman and her horse. The woman, Jackie, was planning on riding the horse, Journey, to the Carolinas. Penny thought about Journey a lot. He had really caught her interest. She could feel that this horse was special. But at the time she and her husband were in the midst of a move to their first farm in Goshen, and she was too busy to do much more than wonder.

Several months later, now settled into the farm, Penny and her husband James were looking for school horses. Penny checked out the ads in the *Bargain News*, where one for a 12-year-old Thoroughbred gelding caught her eye. The ad said the horse was good with kids, an excellent hunter/jumper prospect, and his asking price was $1200. So James and Penny called the Southbury number, and took a drive down to the area for a look.

What they found in a small back yard barn was an extremely emaciated horse. He still had dried sweat marks from a saddle on his back, and was wearing polo wraps. James and Penny were both horrified, and at the same time, intrigued. It was Journey.

Jackie had abandoned the idea of riding him to the Carolinas and taken off for England instead. She had left the horse with a friend for him to sell. Penny wanted to buy the horse just to get him out of the place. The man seemed to mean well, and said he'd had lots of experience with racehorses, but Journey was a mess.

Penny contacted CAP (Citizens for Animal Protection). She had worked with them on a few other occasions. She'd angered the man who had Journey because she had called the Humane Society. After that he stopped returning her calls. Some representatives from CAP went to look at Journey and agreed that the horse was in rough shape.

Penny then had someone she knew from CAP go and buy the horse for her. For $450 she became the proud owner of a six-year-old Thoroughbred gelding who could barely walk 30 feet.

When she got him home, she taped the 16 hand, large framed gelding, at a mere 840 pounds.

Little by little the story of Journey came together. Joe Bills, a farrier who did some of the horses at Penny's farm, was surprised to see the horse. It turned out that he had shod Journey by the side of the road during Jackie's aborted trip. He still had the racing plates that had come off of Journey's feet, and he presented them to Penny. Journey had come from Crowley's, an auction house in Massachusetts that sold a wide range of horses, many right off the track, and many at the end of the line and headed for the slaughterhouse.

Jackie had ridden Journey from Crowley's (and evidently right off the track!) all the way to Wolcott, Connecticut. At night she'd kept the horse in garages, or tied him to fence posts or trees and slept on the ground. The trip took at least a week.

Penny also spoke to the Humane Society, and Karen Hubble, from CAP. Karen had learned from a veterinarian that Journey had been treated for anaphylactic shock following a major overdose of penicillin. Journey suffered from severe abscesses, and had had penicillin prescribed for treatment. Apparently, his owner had misunderstood the dosage by a mile, administering the whole amount she had been given in a single shot. Journey narrowly escaped death.

Through his tattoo, Penny was able to piece together more of the horse's history. His registered name was Night Theatre. A well-bred horse, Journey boasted Bold Ruler in his background. He raced through his five-year-old season as a stallion, running at Suffolk Downs and Rockingham racetracks and winning $28,000. He had bucked shins and was pinfired, but apparently on his return after the pinfiring he wasn't winning, so was gelded and sent to Crowley's.

It took two and a half months of tender care before Journey was ready to be ridden. Penny fed him carefully, increasing his feed gradually so that his digestive system could handle it. Three or four times a day his feet were soaked in hot water and epsom salts, then he was hand grazed and walked. After a month of this, he was able to be turned out. Penny's vet at the time, Dave Sandefer, who Penny describes as an "eternal optimist and all around good guy" only gave the horse a fifty per cent chance of ever being sound.

The horse, however, had other ideas. As he felt better, his personality began to emerge. He would walk out of his stall and climb right into his epsom salt soaks. He was happy that his sore feet were healing, and he loved all the attention he got. He would whinny when he heard Penny (something he continues to do).

Journey also adopted a blue-eyed kitten for some extra company. Murphy, a white mixture of Flame Point Siamese, and domestic longhair, had just come to the barn himself. As the soaking process was beginning to be a tad boring, he and Journey decided to liven it up a bit. While Journey was standing in his soaks, Murphy would sidle over to him. Journey would pick the kitten up and dangle him by his orange ringed tail over the buckets of water, with Murphy purring the whole time. Then Murphy would back slowly down the aisle away from Journey, suddenly rush forward, leap up and grab onto Journey's tail and swing from it. Penny swears she doesn't know how the three of them survived that summer.

With all the love and excellent care, Journey did become sound, and Penny says he was a lovely horse to ride from the start. His walk and canter were excellent, his trot not as good, but still acceptable. Very intelligent, trainable, and comfortable to boot, Journey qualified for the Regional Championships at Training Level in his first year of showing with Penny.

In 1997, he and Penny won the first ever Connecticut Freestyle Championships. It consisted of a series of three qualifiers, one at the Connecticut Dressage Association at Ox Ridge in Darien, one at Mystic, and the finals at the Connecticut Dressage and Combined Training show at Westbrook.

Penny had put together a First Level Freestyle with music by Vince Guaraldi, including some of the music from Charlie Brown's Christmas. The freestyle included such moves as leg yielding, 15 meter canter circles, changes of lead through the trot and lengthenings of trot and canter.

Penny played countless tapes while riding and Journey became very accustomed to standing along the side of the arena while she leaned over to rewind them. While she listened to the music Penny assessed how well it matched his gaits and how he reacted to the music.

The next year, they were reserve champions at the Connecticut Freestyle Championships. Journey's story had gotten around and he had developed quite a fan club!

Journey also has attended Lendon Gray's Young Rider clinics. Penny has to admit that he "will always be my deep down favorite. He's so special and has so much personality."

Journey loves to show and loves to show off. If he's left in the barn when the trailer is loaded for a show, he'll whinny and kick his stall door. "Don't leave *me* out," he says.

The horse who nearly died, who almost starved, and would probably never be sound, had something going for him, something that enabled him to beat the odds. His inherent belief in himself made Journey a winner through it all. This horse *knows* he's something special!

Next time you're tempted to head for Europe for that special dressage horse, take a drive down the road instead. You never know what you may find.

# ⟿ NITRO

They had nothing. Not a dime to their name. They had lost their business and soon they would be losing their home.

The Mancusos had owned a boatyard. It began with big dreams and ended up a nightmare. They'd bought it in 1987, and lived on the property. In 1991, they had to abandon it. The yard was contaminated with Agent Orange. It was a huge loss and bitter disappointment. No one had bothered to inform the Mancusos when they bought it. No one seemed to care that, not only would it wipe them out financially but it would also sicken all of the family. Dee's father, and both of Frank's parents had cancer, cancer that the family believed came about from exposure to the toxic boatyard, where they all had worked.

The Mancusos were devastated, frustrated with the powers that be, and feeling hopeless. They needed something, some kind of change in their lives, something to believe in.

That brown and white Paint sure was beautiful. And fiery. Every time they drove to the barn, he was out in the paddock, snorting, bucking, rearing, and tearing around like a horse possessed.

Frank and Dee Mancuso had come to the barn so that their daughters, Deanna and Theresa, could take pony rides. Deanna, who was 11, quickly outgrew the pony rides and wanted to go for a trail ride. Pelham Bit Farm in City Island had two trails. One went north along the Hutchinson River Parkway and then came back, the other went south along the parkway and then returned.

Deanna got to go on her trail ride. She liked it.

As she and her father, Frank, continued to come to the

barn, they grew to like horses a lot. But they both liked Paints the best.

And they couldn't help looking at that beautiful wild Paint in the paddock.

Frank and Deanna told Dee about the horse. "Ma, you have to go look at this horse," Deanna would say.

One day, Dee asked Frank what the horse's name was. "Twenty-five hundred dollars," was his answer. Horses at Jim Martyn's barn didn't have names. They had prices.

The family was clueless about buying a horse. They didn't know how horses were supposed to behave, or what you would look for when purchasing one.


Dee's father knew how much Deanna and Frank liked the brown and white Paint.

He wanted to buy the horse for Deanna, a parting gift, for he was dying. But he didn't have much money.

Frank wanted the horse, too. He saw how much his daughter enjoyed the horses and he wanted her to have one. It would be nice to have something positive in their lives after all they had been going through.

So Deanna tried riding the Paint. She was small, and a beginner rider, and he was a lot of horse. Too much horse for her, most people thought. But she still wanted him.

Somehow, Frank came up with a $100 deposit for the Paint. Jim would allow him to make time payments. Jim was not concerned that someone else might come up with the full amount for the horse. Everyone thought the Paint was crazy. Besides, two people had bought him, and quickly returned him.

The Mancusos didn't realize that the horse was much more difficult than a new horse owner should ever take on. He was so beautiful and so wild, such a contrast to all they had been dealing with. So the whole family chipped in. Frank, his mother, Dee's mother and father, all contributed. It took two weeks, but they raised the $2500.

The Mancusos now owned that beautiful four-year-old

Paint.

The Paint was so wild that his halter had almost grown into his face. No one dared remove it because getting it back on his head again might prove impossible.

Jim's barn was mainly a sale barn and hack stable, so they moved the horse to a place called North Ridge in nearby Eastchester. It was run by Marie DiSalvo. She seemed knowledgeable and was wonderful with Deanna and Theresa. There were lots of kids at this barn; it had the family atmosphere that the Mancusos wanted.

There were cowboys at the barn, too, men who were there from dawn till dusk. They wore long coats and cowboy hats.

Frank had been a race car driver at one period of his life, driving "funny cars." Nitro is the fuel that makes funny cars go. The paint horse was fast, very fast. So he was named Nitro.

Unfortunately, Nitro was very uncooperative and became more so as he lived at the new barn. He wouldn't let Deanna brush him, pinning his ears and threatening her. He tried to bite people, and kicked an instructor. Once when Deanna tried to ride him, he just stood in the ring for an hour and wouldn't move, reducing her to tears.

The cowboys at the barn all tried to ride him. Everyone *thought* that they could do it, that they would be the one to be successful. Their tactics were rough, their attitude that they would tame that bronc. Nitro dumped them all.

The advice from everyone was the same. "Get rid of that horse." The more people said it, the more stubborn Frank got. He would not get rid of Nitro. He knew what fate was in store for the horse if he was sold.

Besides, under all the gruffness, the horse was sweet. Sometimes when Frank went in his stall, Nitro would lay his head on Frank's shoulder and snuggle.

Finally, one trainer, a man named Raoul, started to make some progress with the Paint. He seemed to know how to get into the horse's mind. Unfortunately he could be severe at times. He used a wire noseband (wrapped in tape) on Nitro. It did do the trick, for Nitro was now at least controllable under saddle, no longer a running, bucking bronc.

Raoul also confirmed Frank's feelings about Nitro. "This is a wonderful horse," he would say, "You just need to understand him."

Deanna worked hard with Nitro. She patiently practiced what Raoul taught her for hours. She would walk Nitro directly at the rail, where he would have to turn left or right. He would choose one direction and Deanna would praise him, and let him think that whatever direction he chose was exactly the one she wanted.

Still, he wouldn't let her brush him or spend time with him in his stall, things the other kids could do with their horses. Nitro would bite, kick, and strike if you went in his stall, particularly if there was food involved, which made him extremely defensive.

One day Deanna rode in a clinic. The clinician chose Nitro, who looked so beautiful standing there, to use as an example. The clinician acted irresponsibly, running his crop across an unknown horse. Nitro protested violently, kicking out and just missing the instructor.

"Get rid of this horse!" he said.

Frank wasn't about to get rid of the horse, but he didn't want his daughter getting hurt either. So he decided that Nitro would be his horse.

He found another horse for Deanna, an old and grubby but very kind black and white Paint. Snickers was headed for the meat truck. Instead he came home with the Mancusos. Now Deanna had a horse she could groom, and take to shows and do all the things the other kids did.

Although the Mancusos were broke, Frank recognized that the horses were crucial to the family's recovery. So they did whatever was necessary to support them. They sold all their possessions: savings bonds, coins, anything they had. Dee's mother waitressed six days a week to help out, and the family used credit cards to survive.

Frank was a rank beginner, too, but he took on the wild horse with the patience of someone who's spent a lifetime with horses. A bit of the horse whisperer, a part of Frank that he probably didn't even know existed, resided in his soul. He spent months doing nothing more than leading Nitro out to some grass and letting him graze.

He would also sit in Nitro's stall, sit there for hours. Nitro got used to his presence and started to play with him. He would grab the zipper on Frank's coat and pull it up and down. If Frank wore anything with strings on it, Nitro would grab the strings and pull them out. It took months, but Nitro began to accept Frank. He learned that this human meant him no harm.

Frank also learned to ride Nitro. At first he would do nothing more than walk. He didn't know how to stop Nitro, so walking was the only safe gait.

One day Frank was asked to join some of the cowboys who were going on a trail ride. Frank told the cowboys he wasn't sure if he should. He only walked, he told them.

The cowboys assured him that that was all they would do.

They were a ways out on the trail when the cowboys took off galloping. Nitro naturally took off after them. Frank could barely stay on, grabbing the horn of the western saddle in desperation. He had never even cantered, never mind galloped.

The trail made a sharp turn, and the cowboys turned with it. Nitro didn't. He kept running, flat out, right onto the Hutchinson River Parkway. He and Frank plunged head first into traffic. Frank was sure he was about to die.

Somehow, he didn't.

Everyone said, "That horse is crazy."

There weren't many people at the barn who liked Nitro; they were all afraid of him. He had to be kept in a separate stall, away from everyone else.

But the man who took care of Nitro, the one who cleaned his stall and brought him in and out, loved him. "This is the best horse in the barn," he told Frank.

Frank had faith in his horse. He didn't know what in Nitro's past made him so angry. He could tell the horse had been lied to and had learned not to trust people. That was something he and Frank had in common.

Frank knew that it was time for him to learn how to ride. He began spending time with an elderly man at the barn.

Mr. Lipper was from Israel, and was in his eighties. When he lived in Israel, Mr. Lipper depended on a horse for his livelihood. It was quite common in his day. His family used their horse to haul junk.

Mr. Lipper had learned a lot about horses, and, coming to this country, had learned a lot about riding as well.

He was good company for Frank, and taught him a lot.

As Frank learned to ride, Nitro's good qualities started to emerge. Barring the first episode, Nitro turned out to be a wonderful trail horse. He became very steady and reliable. Dee, another brand new rider, could take Nitro out on trail and he would not put a foot wrong with her.

Nitro's sense of humor also began to shine through. Frank would tie knots to secure Nitro to something, or in something. Nitro would untie them. Frank could tie knots with the best of them. After all, he'd owned a marina. He tried them all: bowlines, square knots, the toughest knots he could come up with. Nitro untied them all effortlessly.

Once, Frank took Nitro in a "sensory" clinic. The idea was to get horses used to all kinds of things so that they would be unflappable. Nitro already was. Balls were thrown at him, he had to walk across a blue tarp, firecrackers were set off, he even had to walk through fire. Nitro did it all without batting an eyelash.

Although Frank's parents and Dee's father were very ill, they came to the barn when they could. They saw the change in Deanna and Theresa, the happiness that the horses had brought to the whole family. Their gift of the Paint had indeed changed lives.

Nitro had never had an equine friend. He had to be turned out alone because he would either attack or be attacked by whatever horse he was out with.

Deanna's horse, Snickers, changed all that. Nitro accepted him instantly and they became fast friends. Nitro respected, and learned from, Snicker's wisdom. The old horse had a very calming effect on the young one.

The Mancusos had moved from the now abandoned boatyard to a house in New Rochelle. Still, they wanted to put more space between them and this horrible episode in their lives. They'd started looking for a house to rent in Dutchess County, New York. Millbrook was a horsey area with a well kept, never ending trail system (no running into traffic here!) so they had been looking there. They were looking for a while.

It was a good thing that they'd been searching, because they suddenly had to get out of the New Rochelle house fast, with a scant three day's notice. Frank's mother had just died, and he didn't even have the money to give her a funeral. They were only too happy to leave New Rochelle.

Miraculously, a place in Millbrook became available just when they needed it. It wasn't just a house, either. In the back yard sat a three stall barn. The timing on the house was so perfect that Frank felt that the place was a gift from all the family members who had recently passed away.

The Mancusos, Nitro, and Snickers all moved into their new home, leaving behind the pain and tragedy of the past few years.

Now the family could sit on their patio and watch their horses in the paddocks. Life had definitely improved.

One day Frank looked out the window and noticed that, instead of grazing, Nitro and Snickers were standing next to each other, not moving. Nitro had his head across Snicker's back.

Frank went to investigate. He discovered Snickers with his foot through the wire fence. Had he panicked or pulled back, he surely would have suffered a severe injury. But Nitro wouldn't let him. By placing his head across Snicker's back, he calmed him and kept him still until help could arrive.

The sweet horse that Frank had had glimpses of was coming more and more to the surface.

One day Frank and Nitro were, as they loved to do, racing through the trails. As they came to the top of a hill, they encountered some loose gravel. Slipping, Nitro's feet were jerked out from under him. He fell fast and hard, landing on Frank's leg. Nitro was up in an instant, quick to get off of his rider. Frank took a long time to get up, badly injured.

Nitro waited, patiently. Frank couldn't walk. He finally managed to drag himself onto Nitro's back. Nitro carried him home carefully, mindful of Frank's injuries, not heeding the blood that was pouring from his own legs.

Frank had had tremendous patience with Nitro, giving him time and love when anyone else would have quit. Nitro responded. He has become Frank's good friend. There's a difference in Nitro's attitude when he sees Frank, when he hears his voice. Ears that had been pinned back prick forward, eyes soften.

One day Snickers was down. No one could get him up. Frank pulled and tugged, but it was no use. Was this the end for the old man? In desperation, Frank got Nitro from his stall. He asked Nitro to get Snickers up. He was amazed when Nitro bit Snickers hard on the withers and Snickers jumped to his feet. Nitro had finally found a friend, and he wasn't about to lose him!

The Mancuso family had been at their wit's end. Their whole lives had been totally uprooted; they had lost everything.

One spirited brown and white Paint, a Paint who almost lost everything, too, caught their attention. Nitro gave their lives a whole new direction; he was "the glue that kept them all together." The brown and white horse drew them to horses. They came to live in Millbrook where they could keep horses. Deanna chose a career in the horse industry. And the Mancusos started a barn where the whole family pitches in and where they all love to be.

Frank says, "I don't know what would have happened to us if it weren't for Nitro. We didn't know where we would go, what we would do. Nitro showed us the way."

Part of the mission of the barn is to rescue abused horses. For in rescuing those who are unwanted, we often find ourselves.

To find out how you can help the Mancusos help horses, go to www.horsesavers.us or www.luckyorphanshorserescue.com.

# ⤳ Buster Rhymes

He was giving pony rides for a living when Debbie saw him. Just barely surviving in someone's back yard, he was a pile of skin and bones, covered with sores, and about as ugly as they come.

A friend of Debbie's bought the pony, rescuing him from his sad life.

The little gelding was an Appaloosa, with an ugly head and the scrawny tail that often comes with the breed. He was a washed out buckskin to boot. He wasn't really a pony and he wasn't really a horse, measuring 14.3 hands, a hunter/jumper rider's worst nightmare.

Debbie bought him from her friend anyway. He was so ugly he was kind of cute.

She knew she had a client who would lease him. The pony was an excellent mover and a good jumper. He aimed to please, seeming to know that he needed to make up in attitude what he lacked in looks. Debbie found him easy to train and in no time he was jumping around small courses, with automatic changes.

The girl she leased him to did very well at shows and soon they set their goals for the Hampton Classic, a very large and prestigious show held every summer at the east end of Long Island.

Debbie knew he'd be fine, although she had to laugh at the thought of the ugly little horse competing against some of the fanciest, most beautiful, horses in the show world.

She thought, "He's such a good little horse and a good jumper. He does his job. Maybe he'll even bring home a ribbon."

The ugly little horse didn't just bring home a ribbon. With Bucky Reynolds, one of the top hunter judges in the country, officiating, Buster ended up Champion in his division on local day.

Buster's rider next set her sights on the Millbrook Hunter Trials. Millbrook is an area recognized for its horsey residents and expensive and talented horses. The hunter trials were a different test for Buster and his rider. Here they had to negotiate solid cross-country obstacles taken at speed, some with drops, and over varying terrain.

The disdain was so thick when Buster appeared among the competitors that his rider wanted to shrink into the woods. But she was proud of her little horse, and determined to show them all what he could do.

And she did. Buster jumped around like the star that he was, and when all was said and done the scornful riders on their fancy horses had to eat their harsh thoughts. Buster was champion once again.

Remember that song "Never make a pretty woman your wife?" Maybe the same can be said of horses. Buster will never win a beauty contest, but he'll also never stop trying to please his rider. He'll never stop winning either.

# A Gift from a Horse

# ⟿ Soldier: A Horse's Gift

Soldier knew.

We thought we were protecting Alan, protecting his life, but we were actually protecting him from life. We wanted Alan to stop riding; Alan wanted to keep living. Solider came into our lives to teach us all a lesson

Alan was in his eighties and his health unfortunately reflected his advancing age. A series of mini-strokes he had suffered, along with a case of scoliosis, tended to make him list to starboard. But his spirit took no heed of his body's frailty; he was full of life and intended to enjoy every minute of it.

We, the boarders at the barn, were an eclectic mix of people who shared in common our passion for horses. We all loved Alan, and were well aware that beneath that cranky exterior truly beat a heart of gold. It was Alan, along with his wife Nancy, who owned the barn our horses lived in and so we became protective of him.

Alan loved to ride and he especially loved to ride out on trail. Those of us who were pressed into service as Alan's trail guide were warned to do nothing more than a walk. It was just to be a leisurely hack, no craziness allowed. So we would walk sedately out of the barnyard, down the dirt road that followed the course of the river, and out back where the trail climbed for a while up the side of a steep hill. Things would go along as planned until the trail leveled out. And then thundering hooves would be heard as Alan left you in the dust, a blur in the distance if you didn't act fast enough. Sprinting after him on your own mount you would pray that you could catch him before any damage occurred. As you got closer to the blur you could notice Alan leaning to the right and serious panic would set in. What if he fell off? What if he got hurt on your watch?

When you caught up, breathless, Alan would be laughing. "That was great!" he would exclaim while you counted your blessings that everything was okay.

Solider was 10 when he arrived at Hunt Valley Farm. We weren't particularly impressed. The tank-like, mousy brown horse with the big head was a Percheron/Thoroughbred cross and came to us as a replacement for Alan's former mount. Used to gleaming, perfectly proportioned warmblood and Thoroughbred show horses, we at first dismissed him.

However, he was here for Alan, and within 45 minutes of his arrival, five people had tried Soldier. They got on, rode, got off, and handed the reins to another rider. A lesser horse would have gotten cranky. Soldier remained non-plussed. He was being tested and it was obvious that he knew it. We felt that if he could deal with all these different people and their very different styles, perhaps he would be able to handle Alan's less than perfect balance.

Soldier had aced his first test. We knew now that Soldier would probably be all right for Alan, but would Alan be all right with him? We only had to hold our collective breaths for a second, because it was love at first sight. The stout horse that would never win any races or take a ribbon in a horse show took Alan's heart.

Soldier would stand patiently by the mortared stone mounting block while Alan climbed the steps. Alan was slow to mount, his movements hindered by his lack of balance and the stiffness of arthritis. Other horses might well have wiggled and danced, or seized the opportunity to sample the rich grass growing tantalizing near the mounting block. Soldier stood like a rock. When it seemed like Alan was taking forever to get aboard, we would offer our assistance, fearing the horse would grow restless. Alan's stubbornness didn't help. He did not need *us*, he was quite capable of doing it himself, thank you. But Soldier was a saint standing serenely while Alan climbed on, and still patient after a ride when Alan just as slowly climbed off. He grew tall when Alan rode him, moving with the carriage of one who knows he has an important job, and does it with pride.

Alan's bond with Soldier was a crucial part of his life. The horse allowed him to continue an activity he loved to his last days. Those of us who had attempted to discourage Alan from riding because of the decline in his health were overruled by this horse. Soldier refused to see a problem. If Alan slipped toward one side, the horse simply lifted his hip and shoulder on that side, rebalancing Alan in the saddle. If Alan seemed about to fall off at a faster gait, Soldier shifted gear to a slower one. Soldier took over, and taught us to mind our own business.

Alan died recently. His service was mobbed with people there to pay homage to an extraordinary man.

Soldier mourned for his partner. He was retired to horse paradise: a pasture of juicy grass and the company of a pretty mare. He had fulfilled his mission. Like all angels, Soldier had appeared in Alan's life just when he needed him.

And the two of them together taught the rest of us an important lesson.

*Life is to be lived until the day you die.*

# ⌐∴ Perfect

When judges look at a horse and rider, one of the things they consider is how suitable the two are for one another. Coney and Sharon were not. One look at Sharon said athlete. One look at Coney said, "klutz."

He was only seven, a Quarter Horse mix with a heart of gold. His barn manners were good and he was easy to live with. But Sharon was a gymnast, with a body sculpted from years of practice and an urge to excel in any endeavor. She and Coney came to their trainer, Patty Messina, to try to get together as a team, but Patty could see no way to salvage things. It was hopeless. Sharon could never be successful in the competitive show world with this horse. Canter him once around the ring and he would puff like a steam engine. Set up some jumps and he could reduce them to a pile of pick-up stix in the blink of an eye. Patty jumped him over a crossrail once and he stumbled over it, smacking her knee into a standard and leaving her to wonder if perhaps she should carry *him* over the jumps.

Patty didn't know what to do. Coney had to go, but where? If they sold this horse, with no athletic ability *and* a probable un-soundness problem what with his total lack of stamina, what would happen? No one would ever give him a good home. He would end up at the slaughterhouse, and neither Patty nor Sharon could let that happen. He was young and good natured and he deserved a chance at something. They just couldn't figure out what.

Without a lot of hope, Patty placed an ad in *Newsday*, the Long Island newspaper. She was brutally honest about the horse's lack of ability. It wouldn't do anyone any good to varnish the truth. The horse would end up coming back. Besides, Patty had a well-deserved reputation as a reputable trainer and she would do nothing to tarnish that.

Patty only got one call from the ad, which was more than she had expected. A woman named Marilyn wanted a dead quiet horse for her daughter. She had ridden and owned horses herself, so she knew them and knew exactly what she was looking for. She had been searching for nearly a year now and was beginning to think that the horse she needed didn't exist.

When Marilyn arrived, she got on Coney herself, and did some flatwork around the ring. Coney outdid himself, wheezing and blowing after just trotting twice around the small ring. Marilyn didn't ride for long and when she dismounted Coney's nostrils were flaring and his sides were heaving. Patty figured that was probably the end of that. She was sure Marilyn was going to say "No way" and tear out of the driveway.

Instead, she said "I'll take him."

Patty was so flabbergasted she tried to dissuade the buyer. "Don't you want to have him vetted?"

"No, I'll take him."

"But, I really think you should have him vetted." Patty feared that Coney's lack of stamina was a symptom of something serious, and she didn't want him leaving only to return later when Marilyn realized that something was amiss.

"No, Coney is perfect."

Patty's face must have betrayed her confusion.

"You see," Marilyn explained, "my daughter is retarded. She not only needs a horse that won't run away with her; she needs one that can't run away with her. Like I said, he's perfect."

Everything depends on perspective, and Coney, a horse that most of the world would have considered useless, found a niche where he truly was *perfect*.

# ⟶ Oops!

When you absolutely love to do something you don't let a little thing like blindness get in your way.
Rebecca Helman is legally blind. Because of a disease she's had since birth, a degenerative disease which results in macular degeneration, her vision has declined throughout most of her life.

Although the condition now seems to have stabilized, the only remaining vision she has is peripheral.

As a child, Rebecca loved to ride. In fact, she was very competitive, showing in Medal/Maclay classes and the Junior Jumpers. But her vision was pretty good at the time.

Like a lot of people, Rebecca stopped riding when she went to college. Her parents made her sell her horse before she left. The new owners were jumping him in tight quarters when the horse broke his leg. He had to be put down. Rebecca was heartbroken. She swore she would never ride again.

But she never stopped thinking about it. It was a passion, a desire that came from within that would never go away.

In particular she loved jumping. It was a natural high in more ways than one.

So, after being away from it for more than 20 years, and with news of a beautiful equestrian center being built along the Hudson River, Rebecca could no longer resist the call and went back to the sport she loved.

This was one of the first opportunities to re-enter the sport as an adult: a stable that she could reach using public transportation. Rebecca can't drive, so public transportation is her only means of getting places on her own. The equestrian center was called Chelsea Piers and they had a string of school horses that she could ride.

Things had changed since Rebecca was a child. When she

was a kid, her parents paid for everything. Now, as an adult, Rebecca longed for her own horse again. This time, however, the expenses would be hers, so it took quite some time before she was ready to purchase one.

Various circumstances brought Rebecca to numerous stables over the next few years. A trainer at one of the stables had sale horses which Rebecca felt lucky to get to ride. One of these sale horses began to grow on her, but she struggled with taking on the financial responsibility.

In January of 2000 she purchased a flea-bitten gray Thoroughbred named Oops. Oops had been in Pennsylvania doing some upper level jumper divisions. His love for jumping matched Rebecca's.

Once she came to terms with the financial investment, it didn't take Rebecca long to figure out what a good match she and Oops were. Jumping when she had had some degree of normal vision hadn't been that hard. Now, with only peripheral vision to go by, jumping courses became an entirely different challenge. Sometimes she'd steer Oops directly at a standard. He stopped, of course. "You didn't really want me to jump that, right?" he seemed to ask.

It wasn't only Rebecca's love of jumping that made her want to ride again and buy a horse. She simply loves horses. She feels that "One of the most important pieces of riding is the relationship between the rider and his horse."

Jumping for Rebecca has now become an undertaking for three. Not only are she and Oops involved, but so is her trainer, Leslie Bell. Before a class, Leslie and Rebecca walk the course. Rebecca tries to figure out where along the rail she needs to turn. She'll count strides, so for instance she might know that once she jumps the red oxer, she should go four strides, and then make a right rollback turn to the next jump. Leslie works with her to find "tricks that work."

Leslie also accompanies her into the ring, guiding her by voice to help find the natural colored jumps which appear camouflaged to Rebecca.

Rebecca's attitude plays a huge part in the process. "If I stay relaxed, the jumps just seem to happen. If I get nervous, then I start missing."

Doing jumper courses, though it would seem more difficult, is actually easier for her than a hunter course would be. The bright colors of the jumps make them easier to find, and there aren't many straight lines. It turns out to be simpler planning to jump, and turn, jump and turn, than to try to do a line to another line.

Rebecca feels sorry for Oops sometimes, since she often ends up not quite in the right place. But she says, "He's a really good sport. He'll just stop to protect both of us."

Rebecca was so excited recently to not only finish a course at Coole Park, a beautiful facility in Millbrook, New York, but to win. She was almost in tears, and gave all the credit to Oops. "He's got such a great heart. He just keeps going."

The spectators watching the event were thrilled with this wonderful horse and his courageous rider. Oops' great heart and Rebecca's terrific attitude are an inspiration to anyone who sees them.

# KUNG FU

The rain had fallen steadily for days and the ring was slick. The fence heights hadn't changed, however. They were huge. Four foot six to four foot nine, with spreads to the max.

John Blair was sitting on Kung Fu. The pair had gone clean in the first two rounds. They were waiting for their turn at the second jump-off.

Kung Fu had been an amateur jumper rider's mount, one whose rider unfortunately missed quite frequently. He had also been poled a lot and in the process had become quite the tough customer. He was a rough ride, often leaping into the air as he approached the jumps.

Tony D'Ambrosio (Sr.) had bought the horse from his amateur rider. John had seen him go, and was intrigued.

As he'd watched the horse, he'd started to figure him out. When the horse was held back, he rebelled, leaping in the air to show his displeasure. Left alone, the horse would charge toward the fence, and, at the last moment, back himself off. He was a careful jumper who had no desire to crash.

Rodney Jenkins had seen Kung Fu, and he'd said "If you ever get this horse broke, there's nothing he can't jump."

John wanted the chance to see if the strategy he had figured out for Kung Fu would work. He got the opportunity in a horse show at C. W. Post College in Long Island. It worked, and John came home with Kung Fu.

Now here he was at the Brunswick Horse Show outside of Troy, New York. John and Kung Fu were doing well. They'd been in the ribbons all week. They usually were. Kung Fu, a big, powerful and honest horse, was extremely consistent. Anytime John needed money, Kung Fu would go to a show. Every time, he would bring home the bacon.

Wissie Brede was judging that day, and a lot was on the line. The winner of this class would be crowned New York State Jumper Champion. There was a good money prize, and a ceremony and flowers for the winner.

It was their turn. John and the chestnut Quarter Horse entered the ring. They started out clean. But there was a huge oxer to oxer combination by the in-gate. Coming off of the combination, Kung Fu slid in the greasy footing. Skidded out. John's face was inches from the ground, and he was sure that he was about to eat it.

Kung Fu, on his knees, was sliding through the mud. Looking up, John could see the wishing well standards, the bottom rail of the next jump.

"So much for this class," he thought.

But, somehow, they were on their feet! And John was still aboard. Kung Fu was trotting. Trotting towards the massive wishing well jump. John held his breath. They cleared it. There were six more fences. They jumped them all. Clean.

Coming out of the ring, Kung Fu was so covered in mud it was even dripping off his noseband. Wissie looked at the pair. "That horse deserves to win," she said.

John rode away. He was afraid to watch the remaining rounds. He rode back. He was still in the lead.

He rode away again, and again he came back. Another horse had gone. He and Kung Fu still led.

Wissie smiled at him. Kung Fu was still on top. On top despite the fact that he had a club foot, had been nerved in front, and had had a wind operation. But none of that made a difference when a horse had a heart the size of his.

John rode nervously back and forth to the ring until all the other competitors had gone.

Nobody else went clear in the slippery mud. Kung Fu had won the class. He had earned the New York State Jumper Champion title.

John gave his Mom the flowers. She was crying. A lot of people were.

That horse deserved to win.

# ⌁ Redford

A striking gray named Redford is the most popular mount in Lisa Gatti's Pal-O-Mine therapeutic riding program. Redford will take care of the most severely impaired child or adult, yet he is so versatile that he can also make the gifted riders in the program better than they ever dreamed they could be.

Lisa first met the gray gelding when he was at Old Westbury Riding Center. Pal-O-Mine was allowed to rent him for use in lessons. At the time, Lisa's program was in its infancy, and couldn't afford to buy its horses; instead they had to be rented.

Then, the barn closed down and Pal-O-Mine had to move. Even if they had been able to afford Redford, he wasn't for sale. The gray Anglo-Trakehner was very athletic, and had quite the show record. In fact he had been so successful in the jumper divisions that he had competed in The National Horse Show at Madison Square Garden.

Lisa and Pal-O-Mine moved on, but they didn't forget Redford.

In 1998, Amie, the former barn manager for the Old Westbury Riding Center, contacted Lisa. She told her that Redford was turned out, poorly cared for, and needed a good home. Pal-O-Mine was now in a position to own their own horses, and Redford had been a good therapeutic horse. But the owners wanted $3000 for him, and not only was he in poor shape, he was also 21 years old.

That was an awful lot of money for a horse of that age. How many years could he have left? Still, Lisa remembered that he was spectacular looking, and had a marvelous temperament. It couldn't hurt to take a look.

Redford was trailered over to the barn where Pal-O-Mine

was located. He looked dreadful: underweight, shaggy, and with a terribly swollen sheath.

Lisa had to weigh things carefully. Was this horse going to be worth the money the program would have to spend? She decided that he was. She also got a break when Denise Avolio, an instructor for Pal-O-Mine, asked her husband Charlie if Turner Construction would consider helping. Since Denise's husband is Vice President of purchasing for the company, Turner donated the money for the horse.

Redford is used for every evaluation ride that comes in, so every student in the program has ridden him at least once. The gelding has the quality absolutely essential for a therapeutic horse: he is rock steady. He'll stand at the mounting block for the full five minutes that it takes some people to get on him, never moving a muscle.

Keith Newerla, who recently returned from competing in Greece on the Paralympic team, began riding on Redford. He rode the horse quite a while, and Redford taught him the basics of dressage. Together they did first level dressage: bitless. Keith rode him with just a bosal and adaptive reins.

In 2002 Redford competed in the first ever Inner Vision Championships, which was developed by Pal-O-Mine and the National Disability Sports Alliance. Lisa had been equestrian sports technical officer for the organization, until Denise took over.

Lisa and Denise were well versed in the competition arena for riders with disabilities, yet they were upset that no one provided modifications for blind riders. They got the idea of inviting other countries to the U.S. so that they could share their ideas and brainstorm about how to accommodate the blind riders. At the time, Pal-O-Mine was operating out of Caumsett State Historic Park so they had the venue. They needed horses who were qualified for riders up to the Prix St. George level. They were able to borrow 25 horses from along the east coast.

Nine countries competed, bringing riders with varied disabilities. A special division was created for the blind riders, which turned out to be the highlight of the week. Everyone was wowed by these incredible athletes!

Redford's rider had been traumatically brain injured in a car accident. Judy wore a permanent neck brace, was very timid, and had spastic hands. Yet with all these challenges, she and Redford managed to shine. Judy went home with a gold medal for Canada. As Lisa says, Redford always "rises to the occasion."

It's hard to believe that there was a question at first as to whether the horse should be purchased. Redford didn't look like much when he arrived, but when he showed what was inside he proved he was worth the price many, many times over.

People who are blind, people who are in wheelchairs, can ride Redford. He takes riders out on trail. He competes at the prestigious Devon Horse Show in the handicapped class. Redford never takes a bad step.

Lisa's students go to shows where they compete against able-bodied riders. Riding Redford allows them to be on a level playing field with the other kids. Judges don't even realize that kids with disabilities are competing.

Lisa says "He is such an asset to the program. He has a temperament from heaven."

Pal-O-Mine also incorporates hippotherapy in their program, using the horse's movement to influence the rider's movement. One exercise the kids use is riding backwards on the horse and playing basketball. This helps build trunk control. They also do a type of push up, by leaning forwards toward the rump, and then pushing up back off of it. This builds up muscle and strength.

Again, Redford excels. It never occurs to him that all the different positions the kids use while riding him should be cause for alarm.

For the kids, this kind of exercise is fun. It's not therapy; it's recreation. It also helps normalize them. Just like the able bodied kids in the neighborhood, they can play basketball.

Redford, Lisa says, "just goes with the flow. Whatever you want, he'll do it for you."

This past summer, Lisa held a camp at the barn. With 168 kids coming each week, she needed more horses, so she leased some. Unfortunately, one of the leased horses came into the barn with strangles. Horse after horse in the barn came down with it. Lisa was terrified. What if Redford caught it? He had just turned 30. Would he survive?

Redford was the only horse in the barn who didn't catch strangles.

"I'm not going out like *that*," he let them know.

Redford even has been known to bring in extra cash for the program. When Modern Bride wanted to do a photo shoot, Redford was chosen for the job. Not only is he extremely photogenic ("He grows to 18 hands when he sees a camera," Lisa jokes), but with his rock steady temperament, nothing spooks him. The shoot added an additional $1000 to Pal-O-Mine's budget.

Redford also posed with Santa Claus. In fact, Redford is willing to pose with or for anyone. Just point a camera and he'll pose, ears pricked.

Redford has a girlfriend now, a mare named Jeannie. He doesn't let any other horse near her paddock. If she leaves he starts whinnying and neighing, prompting Lisa to say, "I think he's going through mid-life crisis."

Some of his antics give onlookers an inkling of what a handful the handsome gelding must have been in his youth.

Redford has created minor, and not so minor, miracles in his career. Kids have started speaking while riding him. Although moms and dads might find it a trifle disconcerting that their child's first word is "Redford," rather than "mommy" or "daddy" they're still too thrilled to hear that first word to take it badly.

The carry-over to the students' day to day lives is especially rewarding to Lisa, and others at Pal-O-Mine. Behaviors change. Students become more verbal, walk better, become more productive. Redford is a major motivator, a tool for change.

It's obvious to anyone watching that Redford loves his job. The light in his eye, the way he carries himself; this horse knows he's good at what he does, and he loves every minute of it.

Other horses at Pal-O-Mine retire when the time comes, moving on to retirement homes. Redford is the one horse that will never leave Pal-O-Mine. He will live there until he dies (which everyone hopes will be far off in the future) and then he will be buried on the property.

Pal-O-Mine recently received the tremendous gift of having an indoor arena donated to them. A big celebration is planned. As well as celebrating the new indoor, Pal-O-Mine will be honoring Redford's 30th birthday. Redford is symbolic of the organization. For, just as he has come from a neglected, dirty, and malnourished horse to the beautiful star of the program, Pal-O-Mine, too has come a long way, from its makeshift beginnings to its own home-now complete with an indoor arena!

For more information on Pal-O-Mine check out their website at www.Pal-O-Mine.org.

# YOU KNOW YOU'RE HORSE CRAZY WHEN...

## YOU KNOW YOU'RE HORSE CRAZY WHEN...

You open up your coffee grinder to grind up your new hazelnut coffee beans and first you have to wash out the bute.

You can't do your laundry because your horse's wraps are in the wash.

You sneak into a laundromat at 2 a.m. so nobody sees you putting horse blankets in the washing machines.

Your shoes are five years old but your horse's shoes are never older than six weeks.

Your horse gets $300 Rambo blankets, your coats come from a thrift shop.

Your horse gets chiropractic treatments, visits from the acupuncturist and weekly massages, you take an Advil.

You can eat off the floor of your barn, but your house could be declared a Superfund site.

Your spouse knows that he or she is #2.

You don't bake cookies for your kids but you make stud muffins for your horses.

You can't go to your best friend's wedding because you have a horse show that day.

Your saddle cost $3000; your dining room set came from a tag sale.

The only section of eBay you ever go to is Equestrian Supplies.

Your husband automatically pulls over when you see a carriage horse so you can pet it.

There's a saddle rack and neatsfoot oil in your living room so that you can clean your tack while the family watches the news.

You use the same shampoo and conditioner on your own hair as you do on your horse's mane and tail.

Your trophy room is bigger than your living room.

You reach in your pocket for your keys and pull out a hoof pick.

*The new barn at Snowbird Acres with a flagpole for good luck.*

*Dakota and Ann Jamieson competing in the Adult
Amateur Hunters at Coker Farm*

*Tobé Saskor Photo*

*Second Chance and Erica Hughes competing in a show at Tymor Equestrian Center N.Y.*

*City Slicker Luis Reyes and Blanco competing in a jumper class.*

*Ron and Oreo, mounted on Brisa, triumphantly return.*

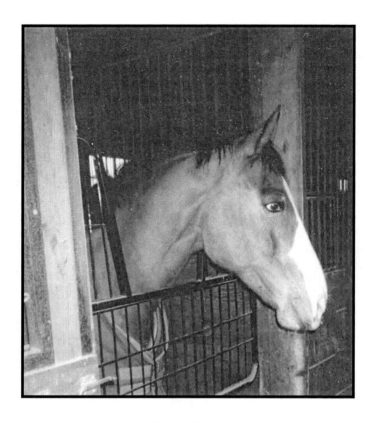

*Victory Tour*

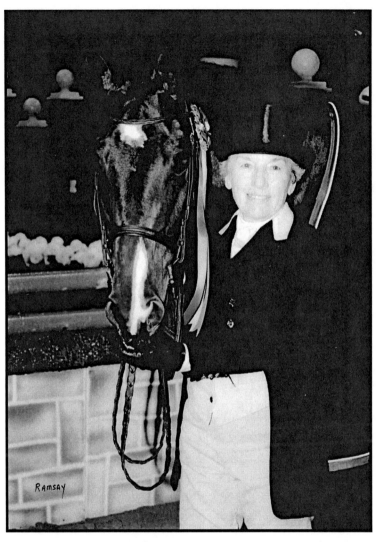

*Betty Oare and Estrella, champions in the Amateur Owner Hunters at the Washington International Horse Show.*

*Teresa Ramsey Photo*

*Iroquois and Allene Simmons on the Grand Prix field in Wellington, Florida.*

*Copyright: Alison Hartwell*
*www.alisonhartwell.com/equine*

# With A Little Help From My Friends

# ⤙ City Slickers

I t all started with a newspaper article. Ruth Fried was reading *The Hartford Courant* in the spring of 1993 when she saw an article that intrigued her. There was a horse farm run by a minority woman, and the woman was inviting people to come ride, people of any race.

Ruth was a schoolteacher, and she was already helping kids by running after- school activities. She took them bowling, or to twirling lessons. But riding? Horses were Ruth's lifelong passion. What a fine idea.

The kids Ruth worked with had never had any contact with horses. Coming from the environment of Hartford, Connecticut's notorious inner city, they were unlikely even to have seen one except on TV.

These were kids who had school problems, problems at home. Ruth's idea was to give them a respite from those problems, a chance to have some fun and relax.

So she took some of the kids to the barn with her. Things clicked immediately. This was where the kids wanted to be. In fact they didn't want to leave.

Ruth started with nothing: no money, no teachers, no barn of her own. Initially, her program was located in the aisle of a former cow barn in Bloomfield, Connecticut. The facility was small, and only had a few horses. That didn't last long. So many youngsters kept asking to participate, youngsters who wanted desperately to ride. Ruth needed a bigger place.

She attended a horse show at Hillside Equestrian Meadows in Wolcott, and was very impressed with the facility. It was a 50 acre site with only two barns when she first saw it. She could see the growth potential there.

Bucky Kalinowski, the owner of the farm, was very supportive. City kids at the barn? Sure, why not.

Ruth had his support and a place to work from. Now she needed some money. She applied for a grant, and she got it. Three thousand dollars.

They had a facility, they had horses (Bucky's!), and now they had money to implement the program.

And soon they had results. Boy did they have results. It was amazing how quickly the horses brought out the best in the kids. Luis Reyes, one of the first students to take advantage of the program, had language problems. He was very quiet and non-communicative.

You'd never know that today. Luis is very expressive and demonstrative, and while he was still in school he couldn't wait to tell everybody there about what went on at the farm.

Luis has gone on to become an accomplished rider and makes his living as a farrier. The program not only gave him a whole new lease on life, but a career as well!

Once City Slickers moved to Hillside, it grew quickly. More kids kept coming, and it seemed as though they were always in everybody's way. They needed their own barn. Ruth got it.

She called Tom Knight, the president of the National Framebuilders Association, makers of wooden frame barns, and explained her dilemma. It just so happened that the association was about to have a convention, and Tom promised he would talk to them.

Shortly after that, Tom called back. "Ruth," he said, "I'm going to make your day." And he did. The association donated all the nails, stall guards, feeders, doors, windows, aluminum siding, and even a cupola. It was basically everything a barn needed except for the wood.

Ruth was on a roll. She called Brescia Building to convince them to do the construction. They agreed to do it at a discounted price. Ruth raised the $15,000 to pay them from the Sally Butler

Grant she received from St. Johns Episcopal Church in Hartford. Now all they needed was the wood. Mike Laureno of Connecticut Retail Lumber Association was the next to get a call from Ruth. He provided her with the association's membership list which included business and contact names, addresses and phone/fax numbers. It made Ruth's job of contacting each member easy and fast. As a result most of the wood for the framework of the barn was donated.

The result was the barn that City Slickers now proudly calls its home. Ten stalls, a wash stall, tack room, and bathroom make up the building.

On a typical day ten to 15 Connecticut schoolchildren converge on the City Slicker barn. They are met by peer leaders: the older, more experienced kids who take on the job of teaching the youngsters. They begin by grooming the horses, learning about them and the vocabulary that pertains specifically to horses, and socializing, One half of the group rides for 45 minutes, while the other half does an "activity." Then they switch. The activity may involve math, or language skills, and ingeniously Ruth teaches these skills using basic horse care. Grain and hay are weighed and measured. Horses are measured for blankets, then the kids are given catalogs. They're taught how to correctly order the blankets. Hands are converted to inches: for example, how many inches high is a 15.2 hand horse?

As City Slickers has grown, so has its staff. Tracie Leach and Lori McVicar are the activity directors and Mike Yorrie is the summer camp director. Gail Corriveau, Ruth's riding instructor, teaches English while Bucky teaches the gymkhana. Bucky's horses have been joined by two that Ruth now owns.

The kids work in the barn on afternoons and weekends, learning to care for the horses and to be responsible for another living being. If they do all their chores on weekends, they earn an extra half hour of riding time.

Ruth has no problem filling any available spots in the program, in fact parents or teachers often come to her with a prospective student. When there are openings, Ruth just calls the District Coordinators, tells them how many openings there are, and they pick the new students.

If any student gets the idea that this program is a piece of cake, they are quickly disabused of that notion. Kids are held strictly accountable for their behavior, and their performance, not just at the barn, but at school and at home.

Students arrive for the first time for one "cycle" (summer, fall or winter). If they stay "on task," they are rewarded by being allowed to return in the spring for ten weeks, and compete in a horse show.

There are schooling shows at Hillside and City Slicker kids get to compete. In addition, all Connecticut Horse Show Association and Connecticut Hunter Jumper Association rated shows include City Slicker equitation and hunter classes in their schedules. These classes are open to all beginner riders: they need not be a City Slicker to enter. Proceeds from the classes go to benefit the City Slicker program.

City Slickers is now in its eleventh year. The program is no longer confined to Hartford. Other districts heard about it and wanted to become involved; it is now a multi-district, urban and suburban program. Starting with a few kids who spent short periods of time at the barn, the program has grown to 100 students in a year-round schedule. The original $3000 grant has been followed by more, and larger grants.

City Slickers has become a state supported activity. Ruth doesn't need to shuttle the kids to the barn any more; now they arrive in the bus that she hired. The program is no longer confined to inner city kids. High needs children from the suburbs also come, and city kids and suburban kids get to know one another, brought together by horses. These kids are all needy in some way, whether it be academically, emotionally or socially.

Ruth, after all these years, does not get paid for her services. She is strictly a volunteer, in it for the opportunity to "bring kids and horses together."

"It's a chance for kids to try something else," she says.

For kids who deem themselves failures it is often their first success. "Horses are great confidence builders for they love and accept them unconditionally."

Ruth continues, "It is a life so different for the tough street kids. Their hard lives are forgotten around the gentle horses. The masks they wear of toughness just melt away in the barn."

Kids are just kids in this neutralizing atmosphere.

Some of the nerdiest kids by teenage standards, the kids that will never be football stars or cheerleaders, find their niche at City Slickers. They get very "tall in the saddle" on a horse. And it rubs off when they're not on the horse, for there is great carry over value for school and for home.

Ruth feels "so lucky to be part of it and so lucky to have such support." She's seen kids who once struggled academically go on to college. One has gone to vet school. Some kids who were abused at home trusted Ruth enough to confide in her. They ended up being removed from the abusive situations and are now in loving, safe, homes.

One child that came to City Slickers had a history of fighting with her teachers. For two years she was constantly suspended. Ruth gave her "tasks." Two weeks of perfect attendance and she would be allowed to sit on a horse. She did it, and she sat on the horse. Then, after two more weeks of perfect attendance, she would be allowed to sit on the horse and walk. She did that, too.

One of the biggest thrills for City Slicker kids is the annual trip to Florida. West Palm Beach to be exact. The big league. Winter in Florida is anybody's dream in the hunter/jumper world, and it's a dream within reach of these once down and out kids.

In order to qualify to go to Florida the kids need to be able to jump a three foot course. Once they can do that, a whole cast of characters gets together to make this dream come true. Eugene Mische, President of Stadium Jumping, who runs the Wellington series, donates stalls, entry and nominating fees, as well as grain, hay, and shavings. Jet Blue comps *all* of the kids' airfare. James Leslie Parker, noted horse show photographer, comps photos for all City Slickers. Equitex made custom show drapes for their stalls; R.O. Landscaping landscaped them. Passersby were so impressed they thought it must be the barn for the USET Olympic mounts!

Frantisi, Classic Coats, English Riding Supply, Devon-Aire, and Toney Equestrian all outfit the riders, from their Grand Prix jackets to GPA helmets. Don Dever Golf Carts donates a nine-passenger shuttle cart. Triple Crown donates horse clothing. Lodging was made available by Palm Beach Community College, which lent its student townhouses. Even restaurants in the area donate the meals.

The kids can't show without trainers, so who trains them? Debbie Stephens, Tim Kees, Peter Trappmann, and other stars donate lessons.

Horses? Some of Bucky's horses go. Some horses, too, are donated. The kids show in children's hunters and equitation as well as schooling jumpers.

These kids are used to the worst that life can dole out. For a few weeks nothing is too good for them. They learn that, as much as people have put them down, or abused them, there are those who want to help. There are horses who give them self-esteem, and a whole new chance in life.

And people like Ruth Fried.

# ⤳ Phoenix

It was indisputably the worst day of Vikki Siegel's life. Her indoor arena and barn burned down, taking three people and 16 horses with it.

At 5 a.m., Vikki had just finished the bookkeeping and did her usual tour of the barn. Everything looked fine. No unfamiliar smells or noises greeted her, nothing unusual caught her eye.

Returning to the house, Vikki was soon in for an unpleasant surprise. It was only 45 minutes later that a worker came to tell her the barn was on fire.

Help came fast. Vikki immediately called the fire department and by the time she put down the phone and walked out the door, the first police car was there and other emergency vehicles were already pulling into the drive.

But it was too late. Everyone inside was already dead. The two workers who lived upstairs and their young baby, Vikki's school horses who were all saints and the crux of her income, and even the beautiful, personable barn cats that everyone at Snowbird Acres had treasured were gone.

Smoke inhalation killed them before the fire got them. In one way it was a blessing, for those on the scene did not have to hear the tortured screams of people and horses being burned alive. But there was no chance for escape, no one to rescue.

The design of the stable, a Kentucky barn, had proved disastrous. With stalls in the middle and a track around the outside, a draft had formed which created a fireball inside. No one could have survived.

No one who was there will ever forget the sight of the last

barn cat, digging frantically in the ashes. Apparently she had left the barn to forage for her new kittens. She returned to find her cozy home reduced to nothing but hot, blackened ashes. Trying desperately to find her kittens, she didn't stop digging for two days, until her paws were raw. Her plight was symbolic of the whole tragedy. Where did everybody go? How could they all disappear?

What do you do when lives, and your life's work, go up in smoke in minutes? No one unfamiliar with fire could believe how quickly everything was gone. Nothing but the chimney remained standing. The young couple who had worked for Vikki were gone, along with their baby. A 200' tree located near the barn stood scorched to the top. The tack room with all the bridles, saddles, and supplies for the school horses, the indoor arena, the trophy room with a 15 year collection of silver trophies, championships and blue ribbons had all vanished.

The "working" horses that they lost, the schoolies, were part of the family. The best school horses you could find had lived in that barn. Trigger could take students from leadline to the outside course and everything in between and win it all. Playmate, a pony, would go to the shows and beat Dresden, who was a national pony champion year after year. Many had been state champions and had encouraged new riders to be better than they ever thought possible.

Vikki and her family were ready to give up. Collect the insurance money and call it quits. How could they go on?

The media were horrible, all over the place, haunting them when they needed peace. Reporters wanted burned bodies for their stories. Vans, helicopters, covered the place with newspaper people, TV people from every station and every paper. Literally, they were crawling on the rooftops. It was one of the biggest stories in the country.

Vikki worried. Were they going to wind up in jail? The arson squad dug for evidence in the embers, trying to reconstruct the fire.

What happened? Did the furnace go bad? Did mice chew through electrical wires? Had pigeons nested somewhere, causing a short circuit? Would the Siegels be found guilty of negligence? If they were, who would go to jail? What would happen to the children? The other horses? Question after question raced through their minds.

The family that had lived above the barn, where were their relatives? Vikki had no idea who to call. How could she notify their families?

They felt defeated, they wanted to just give up. They *would* have given up.

Vikki, despondent and in mourning, sat in the house refusing to answer phone calls. She did not want someone calling to commiserate with her. One person kept trying to get through. Vikki wouldn't talk to him. She didn't want to talk to anyone.

George Tauber was persistent. He *had* to get through. Eventually, he did. "Do you have a Miller's catalog?" he asked Vikki. At the time, Miller's was one of the largest horse supply companies in the country.

"Yes," Vikki replied. Sure she did. Any stable had a Miller's catalog on hand.

"Pick it up and go through it," George told her. "Make me a wish list. I want you and your daughters to sit down and pick out everything that you need to restart your business. Anything you want, anything you need, make a note of it. And I'll try to see if I can put together what you need."

Vikki was stunned. Instead of dwelling on her losses, here she was with her two girls going through a Miller's catalog. She realized the extraordinary gift George had just given her. It wasn't just the items in the catalog, although that was tremendous. The bigger gift was the gift of an option, of opening a window that wasn't there for them before. Maybe they *could* pick up and continue, with a little help from their friends. The end of the road was now a brand new starting point. George took the Siegels from depression and hopelessness to planning for the future, "the most beautiful thing anyone could ever do."

That was the turning point.

After that, amazing things continued to happen. Many

towns are hostile to horse farms and are only too happy to shut them down when given the chance. Vikki didn't have a dime, and Washington could easily have closed her doors after the fire because the farm had been grandfathered in. Instead, the town did everything it could to help them get back on their feet. The community stood behind them one hundred per cent.

The arson squad found the Siegels innocent of any wrong doing. Their investigation led to a recounting of the events of the fire. Apparently, the young man had gotten up to hay the horses, and put on coffee before leaving the apartment. He dropped the hay in the hay drops, and by the time he returned, the stove was on fire. His attempt to douse it with a water hose proved futile.

The saddest thing was that there was a window in the apartment bedroom that could easily have been opened, and it was only an eight foot drop to the ground. The bedroom also led to the hayloft, which was the last part of the building to burn. A ladder coming down from the hayloft would easily have led them to safety.

The young family's relatives were located from the license plate on their car. And Vikki learned an important lesson, one all barn owners should keep in mind: always know how to get in touch with the next of kin of your employees.

Soon things started arriving. Miller's, good to their word, delivered on the wish list. Buckets, blankets, tack, even horses showed up. Vikki didn't even know many of the people who donated items. But they had heard, and they wanted to help. The very first person to call her was someone she had never gotten along with particularly well. She certainly would not have expected him to help. He called to offer her a horse through the next summer.

More phone calls came in. "I have a horse I'm not using right now. Can you use it?"

Another beautiful gift came from George's wife, Chrystine. She worked for the USET and donated blankets from the USET's horses to the school. How exciting for kids who were in shock over losing their beloved friends, to have blankets that had been on Olympic champions!

The barn that housed the private horses, thank God, remained unscathed. But how was Vikki going to buy their feed? The fire happened on a Monday; on Wednesday Snowbird Acres planned to have a horse show. Could they hold it? How would that look? But if they didn't, how would they reach people and tell them not to come? And more importantly, if they didn't, how would they raise the money to continue?

They did hold the show. Shortly afterwards, at another show, Frank Chapot overheard someone complaining about the Siegels. "How could they hold a show after they just had that fire? After people died?" the person asked. Frank spoke up. "How do you expect them to feed the other horses?"

The Professional Horseman's Association and the New Jersey Horse Shows Association waived all fees for holding their classes at Vikki's shows for a year.

An old-time farmer named Fred who worked for Vikki kept everything working and moving when no one else would have been able to do so. His years of farming gave him the knowledge of how to fix things that would have been way too costly to replace, or that couldn't have been replaced at all.

Everyone who pitched in, pitched in casually. No one made a big deal out of what they were doing, instead they acted as though this was what you would do, no question, automatically. Vikki's mom had always told her "Doing something good is expected, it's not noteworthy."

That spirit was just what came to light in the wake of the fire. The Siegels had been knocked down and the horse community had rallied to get them back on their feet. That was precisely what made the Siegels decide to continue. If all these people had come forward to support them in their time of need, the Siegels felt, then they must have been doing something right.

The new barn is nicer than ever. The apartment is now separate. A sophisticated security system is in every barn, and fire drills are practiced regularly. A year after the fire, seven cartons arrived from Miller's. Bridles, saddle pads, buckets, galloping boots, all of Miller's close out items were shipped to Snowbird Acres.

George Tauber is now mayor of Tewksbury. He was elected on a ticket of making the town a horse community.

For a brief moment, Snowbird Acres' future hung in the balance. That balance shifted when the love of friends, neighbors, and flat out strangers gave them the will to go on.

# ⤳ Teamwork

The girl must be dead.

Janice Callahan had never seen such a bad accident in all her years of teaching. Jenn, a student on the University of Connecticut's intercollegiate riding team, had missed the distance to the jump, asking the horse to take off far too early. The mare couldn't make it, and her two front feet clipped the top rail, causing Jenn to catapult over her horse's head and land face first on the other side. The horse, out of balance and with nowhere else to go, landed on Jenn. It was muddy and as the mare tried to regain her balance she slipped, falling on Jenn again.

Janice could see that Jennifer wasn't moving. There was no sign of life in her. Janice was afraid to approach, afraid that the young girl might be dead. But she had look, and the sight seemed to confirm her worse fears. Jenn lay still, with blood pouring out of her mouth.

An ambulance had already been called.

Jennifer wasn't dead. But, her ribs had been fractured, she was unconscious, and her lower lip had been ripped severely. Black lines of dirt were etched deeply into her face, evidence of how hard it had been driven into the ground. It took 32 stitches to put her mouth back together, and a year after the accident Jennifer needed plastic surgery to remove the lines from her face. Most of all, the emotional repercussions continued long after the physical scars had healed.

The accident didn't shake Jenn's love for horses. Only a week later, she was back at the barn, visiting her own horse. Jenn

*123*

had started a two year old filly named UConn Black Raspberry in a training class at school. The first semester consisted of ground work and lunging lessons. The second semester Jenn continued work with Razzy. She fell in love with the beautiful young filly and bought her. Razzy was small but full of love, a real personality kid. Her coat was a polished black and she had red/black highlights in her tail that inspired her name.

Unfortunately for Jenn, being at the barn that first week out of the hospital was torture. She wanted to ride again. Maybe, she thought, she could ride a quiet school horse. She asked Janice if that would be okay. Janice said yes, and Jenn rode. But fear gripped her. Her confidence on the flat returned quickly, but she couldn't help but have flashbacks of her fall. She was afraid of jumping.

She knew she had to get past it. So she took the school horse, Clarence, over a tiny ground pole. That went all right, so she tried a tiny cross rail. She did this twice in each direction, and called it a day. "At least I had gotten back and jumped immediately," she thought. The jump was so small that Clarence trotted over it. But it was a first step back into jumping.

Driving home that night, her ribs sore and the stitches irritating her mouth, Jenn thought about how differently she now viewed jumping. Once it had been an adrenaline rush, a natural high. Now it was a fear that she must continue to stare in the face until it went away.

She continued to school at least one horse per day at the University of Connecticut. In addition, she was back on Razzy every morning.

Two weeks later Jenn decided it was time to get back into lessons. She was feeling pretty confident on the flat, and thought she was capable of doing a jumping lesson. Yet, when it came time to jump something beyond a small crossrail, the butterflies returned full force. Jenn was terrified. Riding was her future, her life. She had to do this, to push past her fear. She forced herself to trot to a fence. Her horse stopped. Jenn hit the ground and was so shaken she started crying.

How was she going to overcome her nerves and her fear, she wondered? It had taken so much to get on and jump again after her accident, and the outcome had been that she'd fallen once more. Trying to get past her fear, she had instead reinforced it.

A lot of people would have given up. Jennifer didn't. She couldn't. "Riding and horses are my number one passion," she says. She knew that, "If I don't overcome my fears now, I never will."

She got right back on the horse, wiped her eyes and took the fence.

This time horse and rider landed safely together on the other side.

Janice was a huge help. She gave Jenn difficult horses to ride in flat lessons as well as just to exercise. This enabled Jenn to continue to advance in her riding, getting lots of confidence building hours in the saddle without having to constantly face her fear of jumping. Jenn also moved down from her advanced level class to an intermediate level for a while, so the smaller jumps would not be so intimidating. When Jenn began jumping consistently again, Janice made sure she rode the "honest" horses that would take care of Jenn over fences. Gradually Janice gave her the harder horses, when she felt she was confident enough to handle them.

Janice encouraged her, pushing her in a positive way, telling her she could do it without overfacing her.

Jenn's teammates pitched in as well. Jessica Salonia helped her by setting up jumps and encouraging her. Jessica achieved a major breakthrough with Jenn when she set up one tiny jump and said "You can do this, just this." She told Jenn, "Don't think about a course, don't think about the jumps, all I want you to do is get a perfect distance to this little fence." Jenn did. Jessica raised the fence, a little at a time, always reminding Jenn to forget a course, just get the distance to this one fence.

These building blocks helped Jenn little by little build up her confidence. Jenn was back in the advanced lessons exactly six months after that breakthrough day.

Meanwhile, Jenn had been working with Razzy again. Razzy was her trusty ride. She would take her on trails in the woods and riding her was always pure heaven. Together they explored the beautiful Connecticut countryside. They would go on moonlit walk rides when the full moon was out. These were the rides when worries were non-existent. Razzy was Jenn's best friend and she spent all of her free time at the barn with her. She and Razzy were very close, they had been together from the start and Jennifer had been the first one to ride her. They were working to build a team and the bond between them was obvious to all. Jenn was excited about their future. She planned to do hunter paces and local shows with the mare, to just enjoy her. Razzy, she thought, was going to be "my girl, my horse for life."

And although Jennifer was no longer the fearless rider she once had been, she was feeling stronger all the time, getting her life and her future career back on track. And Razzy was the one horse she had complete confidence in.

Then, Razzy colicked. It didn't seem bad when it started, at eight in the morning. So Jenn walked her mare for hours. But by the third vet call, at 11 p.m., nothing had improved. Razzy was rushed to Tufts. After checking her carefully, no one could be sure what had caused the colic, but surgery gave her only a 30 per cent chance of survival. The other option was to keep her there for three days, while she was watched and walked by the Tufts' staff, and see how things progressed. It was a difficult decision.

After listening to the advice of the on-call vet, Jenn decided on the latter option. They would try monitoring her first before resorting to surgery.

For three days, they walked and treated her. Jenn was not allowed to stay with her horse, but she did come every day to see her. Things were not going well. There was no improvement.

Jenn awoke at 5 a.m. on the fourth day to a phone call she will never forget. It was the vet that had been caring for Razzy at Tufts. "We're putting her down," he told her. "She is in too much pain." Jenn never even got to say good-bye.

Jenn was overwhelmed. She had come back from a devastating fall and was still working hard to regain her confidence. Now her beloved Razzy was dead and there wasn't anything Jenn could have done to save her. How could she survive this blow?

She kept blaming herself for Razzy's death. "Why didn't I have them try surgery on her? Why couldn't I save her?" Her mother consoled her by saying "If they had done the surgery and she had survived she may not have been the same healthy horse. She may have had more problems down the road. Everything happens for a reason, Jenn."

Nothing made Jenn feel better. No words could help.

Jenn had lost Razzy, but her team came through for her once again.

They did everything they could to ease her pain. A ceremony was held at the University of Connecticut. Janice, along with Jenn's teammates, planted a tree in Razzy's honor. The girls brought her flowers, and supported her in her successful bid to become president of the Intercollegiate team.

Jenn not only lost her baby, but now she had large vet bills to pay, bills that were especially hard for a college student to cover.

Janice knew that besides being a good rider, Jenn was a good student who maintained above average grades. She helped Jenn get an intercollegiate scholarship for $800 to pay those bills.

Jenn was extremely grateful for Janice's help, and for her teammates. She didn't know how she would have made it through if not for this group of people who cared so much, and helped her through this disastrous period of her life.

Jennifer has since graduated and now has three horses of her own: two of them are black Morgans. With the help of her teammates and her coach she was able to overcome her fear and her loss, and pursue her passion.

Her dream is in progress. Jennifer just bought 18 acres to build her own barn where she will teach riding and start young horses.

# Guidance

The horse would not pick up the right lead.

No matter what Richie Fisher did, it didn't work. The horse just wasn't going to pick up that lead. Okay, so on occasion he did. For one stride. And then it was gone. He'd swap right back to the left lead.

Richie didn't know what to do. He'd been training horses for years. Getting one to pick up a certain lead had never been such an issue.

He was frustrated and didn't know what to do next.

He rode the horse into the center of the ring and just sat there. And prayed. He asked the Lord, "What do I do? I've tried everything to get this horse to pick up the right lead. Tell me what to do."

The answer came. "Blindfold his left eye."

It seemed a bit unusual, but it was clear that that was what the Lord wanted him to do.

So Richie blindfolded the horse's left eye. He put a gauze pad over it, then wrapped it on with a leg wrap. It caused a bit of a stir, as the horse looked like it had just come out of surgery. Everyone asked, "What are you doing?"

Richie worked the horse slowly in his blindfold. He walked for a while. Then over a few days he walked and trotted: always to the right. After four days of this, he felt comfortable enough to ask for a canter.

The horse picked up the correct lead to the right. And stayed on it. All the way around the ring.

The next day he picked up the right lead again. Richie pulled a tiny bit of the blindfold away from the eye, and continued riding only to the right.

Day by day, he pulled a little bit more of the blindfold back. Eventually the horse had full use of the left eye again. And he still picked up, and stayed on, his right lead.

Richie never had a problem with him with the right lead again.

He has used that technique ever since. If a horse has a problem in one direction, Richie blindfolds the opposite eye. Of course, the blindfolds have advanced over time. No longer do the horses end up looking like accident victims. They now wear racing blinders, modified with a full cup that completely covers the eye.

It works opposite sides of the brain control opposite sides of the horse, for example the left brain controls the right side.

Even teaching a horse to spin, the technique works wonders. If a horse spins well in one direction, but is sloppy in the other, the blindfold soon has the horse spinning equally well to both sides.

The Lord answers all prayers. You just need to be open enough to listen.

# SURPRISES

# ⤳ Nikki's Dream

Working on a horse farm was good and bad. You got to meet a lot of different horses, work with them, and ride a lot.

The problem was, when you fell in love with one, you had to watch it go off to a new home and leave you behind.

Nikki loved her job. It was hard work: doing stalls, walking horses back and forth to their paddocks, feeding, and watering. She had to lift heavy buckets of water and bales of hay. She even helped load the loft after haying sometimes, dragging bale after bale off the trucks and putting them on the conveyor belt to go up over the barn. This work could go on for hours in the brutally hot sun. And it didn't mean a break from her regular duties, this was in addition.

The horses made it worth it. She loved to watch them play in their paddocks, and she loved to listen to them munching on their hay in their stalls at night. They were beautiful, and they were a lot of fun.

She had had a couple of her own horses for a short while, but none were the right match. Roo was small and very limited in his ability, so Nikki couldn't progress in her lessons. She traded him in for Bailey, a chestnut Quarter Horse. But Bailey liked to buck her off, and do it dangerously close to the walls of the indoor, giving her parents and anyone else watching, heart failure. It didn't bother Nikki. She would get back up and get right on again.

Then there was Priscilla, a pretty mare but one who had soundness issues.

So Nikki was without her own horse now. She wanted one. But it wasn't so bad when she had all these horses to ride.

Sale horses came and went frequently at the barn. Most of them didn't catch Nikki's attention. Some were cute or personable, but none of them seemed outstanding. Then one day she overheard her boss, Carol, on the phone talking to a horse dealer. Two new horses were coming. Carol told her to make up some stalls for them.

The next morning Nikki arrived at work, eager to see what had come in, yet not expecting much. When she got to the stall where one of the new horses was, she couldn't believe her eyes. There stood "the most beautiful creature I had ever seen." Named Black Angus, he was a gleaming black Thoroughbred/warmblood cross with a white star and snip. It was cold at the barn, early spring, and all the other horses were outfitted in their shaggy winter coats. Angus, arriving from Ocala, Florida, was resplendent in his summer tuxedo.

Nikki opened his stall and looked closer. He appeared to be a little over 16 hands. He came right over to her, impressing her with his friendly attitude. They bonded instantly and Nikki knew beyond a shadow of a doubt that she wanted this horse more than anything she had ever wanted in her life. It was love at first sight with this handsome stranger.

Already Nikki could hear Carol on the phone, letting people know that she had a nice horse for sale. "*Nooooo!*" Nikki thought. She couldn't bear to watch him climb onto a trailer and go where she would never see him again. What was she going to do? His price tag, $7500, was much more than her parents had spent on a horse before. Roo, Bailey, and Priscilla had all been in the $1500 range, a fraction of what Carol wanted for this horse. There was no doubt he was worth it. The seven-year-old gelding had good looks and several years of training: he could go far. Nikki thought, "they" could go far. She wanted a horse that she could advance with, and take to shows.

One of the older girls at the barn gave Angus a test drive. She jumped him around a 2'6" course and Angus loped easily over the fences. His flying changes were automatic. His schooling had been well planned and thorough.

People came to look at Angus. Several people. Some came

close to buying him. It tortured Nikki. Every time someone came she would have to get Angus ready. She was the one who would bathe him and brush his gleaming coat to perfection.

Nikki would tell her parents over and over again, every day, how much she wanted the horse. Yet she knew he was out of their price range.

Then one day a little girl came to look at horses. She tried two of them and one was Angus. She wanted him and planned to move him to a new barn. It was quite a distance from where she lived, and she would only be able to visit him on weekends. Nikki was so sad. Angus wouldn't have a life. There wouldn't be anyone there to love and be his owner. The little girl left, very happy, with plans to buy Angus.

A few days later, the family came back again. They tried him again, and again, things went well. As they left, Carol reminded them, "You need to call me no later than at 3:00 today, or I'll start showing the horse to other people."

They didn't call and they never came back.

Nikki was ecstatic. She was saved. But how many times would she be lucky?

She cried to her parents again. "Please buy me this horse. I want this horse so much."

Sandy and Kevin Irish wondered what it was about this horse that had so caught their daughter's attention. They thought it was just a phase, a phase that would pass. Sandy felt Angus was pretty, but didn't think he had much personality. And she told Nikki to quit dreaming because Angus cost too much money.

Kevin felt the same way. "What does she need this horse for?" he wondered. "She likes all horses. This one's too expensive."

Nikki understood her parent's reservations, but she didn't stop dreaming. The bond between her and Angus was too strong. She *had* to have this horse.

She went to Carol and told her how she felt. Maybe she could take some lessons on him and see how it went? Carol agreed. Carol thought Nikki liked Angus only because of his good looks. Nikki explained to her that that was just the start. Sure, he was beautiful, but he was also a horse that she could learn on. With his experience, he could improve her riding. She could advance on him, and go to shows.

Nikki rode Angus, and the lessons went well. Very well. Ike, the instructor at the barn, told her parents that Nikki and Angus formed a good team.

Carol tried to steer Nikki to other, less expensive horses. There was Baron, a big good looking chestnut. Baron also had quite a bit of training. Unfortunately, the training had taken place years ago and he was so rusty it took a rider with a lot more experience than Nikki to dig deep enough to find it.

There were some small pintos and Appaloosas and other horses at the barn too, but none had the charisma or ability of Angus. They were basically for people who just wanted to trail ride every now and then. Nikki didn't want them, she didn't want Baron.

She wanted Angus.

The night before Easter, Nikki and her family planned to go out for dinner. Kevin was nowhere to be found. Unbeknownst to Nikki, he was paying a secret visit to the barn. He did arrive back home and the family went out for dinner, but Kevin was mysteriously silent about where he had been.

Nikki cried all that night, she was so disappointed that this wonderful horse was not hers.

On Easter day Carol told Nikki that a lady was coming to look at Angus and that she needed to clean him up.

Nikki prayed that the woman would not want him. The torture was getting harder and harder for her to bear. She saw Angus coming in from the field, covered with mud and dirt. She was secretly happy that he looked so awful at the moment. Carol told her since he was so dirty maybe they should give him a bath. Nikki thought maybe if he stayed dirty the woman wouldn't want him.

Instead, they just groomed Angus and put him in his stall. When they did, Nikki noticed an envelope sitting on a blanket on his stall. Nikki's name was on it.

She opened it up. The letter inside said "Nicole, you will

have to start cleaning this stall for the horse in it right now belongs to you."

Nikki didn't know what to do. She turned around and saw that her parents had come in and were watching her. Running to them, she gave her parents a huge hug. Tears rolled down her face. Tears of amazement, tears of gratitude. Her dream had come true. This was the best present she had ever gotten.

Kevin and Sandy got creative when they realized the extent of their daughter's attachment to the big black horse. They knew it would devastate her if Angus left. Kevin's Easter eve excursion to the barn had been to talk terms with Carol. She had agreed on time payments.

Angus is Nikki's best friend now, her life. She's with him every day, and they go to horse shows and hunter paces and trail rides. They've become a beautiful team, one of those perfect matches of horse and rider that judges love to see. Nikki's friends think she is strange because she doesn't hang out with them. She's always with her horse. But none of them "know how it feels to love an animal so much. If they did, then they would understand how I feel...I'm just so happy to say I own a horse and I love him very much. He is my dream come true!"

# MARRY ME

Jennifer was in a hurry. She had to be at work by 7 a.m and she still had the stall to muck.

She wondered why Tony was hanging around. What was he up to? Couldn't he see she was busy?

They had been seeing each other for over a year now, and sometimes Tony would come with her to the barn in the morning. He took care of some heifers at nearby Sunny Valley, just down the road.

Jennifer loved having him there with her. But today, she was in a hurry.

Behind the barn there was an area full of trees, pricker bushes, and brush. It wasn't a space you could turn a horse out in, but there were trails in it and sometimes it was fun to ride through.

Tony had been working on the area a lot, pruning and cutting and clearing. Jennifer knew he'd spent a lot of time there the day before but she didn't give it much thought.

Tony had been doing more than clearing in the woods: he had carved trees, bushes and even prickers when there was nothing else that would work, into letters. "This is for the easy parts," he thought as he carved trees and bushes, "and this is for making it through the hard times," as he neared the end, chopping away at rough pine and pricker bushes, trying not to get scratched.

But now Tony was bugging Jen to look out at the trees, bugging her when she was afraid she would be late to work.

"Look out back," he told her.

"Yeah," Jennifer said, unimpressed. It was pretty, the valley and the trees. But she had seen it before.

"Look at the deer out there."

"Where?"

"Don't you see it over there? The big buck."

"I don't see a big buck," Jennifer said, confused. What was he looking at? But then she did see something, although it wasn't making a whole lot of sense to her. It was an "M," carved out of part of a tree and some bushes.

What, she wondered, was that about? "I do see an M," she said "What else do you see?" Tony asked. "Look some more."

Jennifer looked harder. She saw an "A." She kept looking. "I see an "a," and an "r," and another "r."

She kept going. "Marry me," it said.

Jennifer turned and looked at Tony. She couldn't help it, she was crying.

"Yes, I will," she told him.

And she did.

# ⤙ Lil Abner

The snow was deep, up to their knees. Maybe not deep if you lived in Wisconsin, but for Long Island it had been quite a snowfall. And the drifts in places could easily hide a car.

It was the perfect setting for the Christmas postcard, a Thomas School of Horsemanship tradition that dated back to the beginning of the school's history. And what better subjects for this postcard than the four old timers? With an average age close to 30 among them, this quartet had taught hundreds of kids to ride.

They were turned out on the hunt course, a huge field off to the side of the barn. Like kids let out for winter vacation, the snow beckoned them. "Playtime!" it announced. And play they did, despite their age.

Nancy Thomas, the owner of the barn, and her manager, Judy, had turned them out and then stayed a bit to watch the theatrics. The horses strutted their stuff, passaging and pirouetting in the snow, heads high, tails proudly arched. Their breaths could be seen from a distance as they snorted in the chilly air.

Lil Abner, a large big boned pinto, was especially proud of himself. Abner had been purchased as a three year old, and despite his build, always carried himself beautifully. He was sure he owned the farm, and walked around the place commanding anyone in his presence to "Look at me!"

But Abner had run all the way to the farthest edge of the field, almost out of sight. And when Nancy and Judy turned to see where he had gone, their hearts sank. All they could see were four legs sticking straight up in the air.

"Oh my god," they thought, "he's had a heart attack and

died. And he is already in rigor mortis, all legs stiffly pointing to the sky." The joy of seeing the horses playing in the fresh snow was rapidly eclipsed by their fear of what had happened to Abner.

Nancy and Judy began running towards the horse, terrified at what they would find. The deep snow slowed their progress. Their hearts raced in their chests, their legs burned, and soon they began to think *they* would be dead before they got to him.

As they approached Abner, they looked at each other. What would they find? Would he still be breathing? Their progress slowed. Neither was sure she wanted to know.

At last they were close enough to take a look. Together they peered cautiously at the big horse. And in unison they sighed.

Abner, it turned out, was not dead, merely stuck. A hearty roll in the heavy snow had somehow left the horse wedged in this awkward position.

His sides were rising and falling in labored breathing, but breathing it was. Smiles lit up reddened faces and the two immediately set to work to right the upside down horse.

The perfect photo opportunity did come up. Despite the odds, the four old-timers decided to pose together in the midst of the snow covered field, creating a charming Christmas print. And Abner, standing in the middle of them, was smiling. Laughing at them. "Gotcha," he seemed to say.

# ⟶ KAYENTA

A young doctor was doing his orthopedic residency on a Navajo reservation, Kayenta, in Northern Arizona. He had grown up in the crowded suburbs of the East and relished being out in this remote area. He described it to his friends as the middle of nowhere and he wasn't exaggerating. The closest village was 70 miles away; the closest town was over 140 miles away.

This part of Arizona, known as the "four corners" area (where Arizona, Utah, Colorado and New Mexico meet), is dramatically beautiful. Buttes rise up several hundred feet in the air, and interesting rock formations can be seen in every direction.

The Indians here lived off the land, and the land was lousy. Most were supported by the government. Some, those that were somewhat more well off, had horses, There wasn't a lot to be proud of on this reservation, but the horse owners were lucky. The horses were a source of real pride to them.

When the doctor was about half way through his residency, he treated an elderly Indian who had broken his leg. He put the man in a cast and told him to come back in six weeks so he could take the cast off.

Six weeks later, there was no sign of the man. In fact, months later the doctor still had not seen him. He couldn't understand it. What would make the man keep from returning to have the cast removed?

Finally, six months later, the doctor was driving around the reservation in his jeep. He spotted the old Indian riding his horse. The cast was still on his leg.

He drove up to his patient.

Getting out of the jeep, he asked him, "Why didn't you

come in so I could take your cast off?"

The answer was alarmingly simple. "Because I ride much better with the cast on."

# ⤙ THE PINK PONY

With four young daughters who all wanted to ride, Marianne Savino decided the family needed a pony. They were new to the horse scene so they went to a large and respected sales barn near their Center Moriches, New York, home. There they purchased Cloudy from Ralph and Holly Caristo. The gray pony was eight, a scant 11 hands, with the unmistakable pony face that meant trouble was brewing.

Cloudy, like many ponies, was dressed for winter with a thick fur coat. The Savinos had no barn at the time, just a field with a run-in shed. (The fields are now home to the Savinos' Salt River Farm). So Cloudy lived outside and grew shaggier. His mane grew long, stretching down almost to his shoulder. Clip him? Pull his mane? No one knew about these things.

In the early spring Marianne decided it was time to go to a horse show. She found one not far from their Long Island home, at a place called Equitation Lodge.

Cloudy would need a bath, so that meant he would need a blanket. Red, they decided, red would look good on a gray pony. So they ordered one for him. It was custom made, because of his small stature, and everyone was anxious to see how he looked in it.

The night before the show, Marianne and the kids gave Cloudy a bath together. They were all excited about the show and did a good job of scrubbing the pony. When they finished, he was clean, but his long hair was still wet.

Next, Marianne braided him. She had never braided a horse before but she knew that that was what you did for a horse show. With his long mane it wasn't easy. The braids turned out thick. And they didn't lie flat. Little gray sausages popped up along Cloudy's neck.

The red blanket on the gray pony looked adorable. It fit perfectly, and even dressed him up a bit. Cloudy was turned back outside in his new apparel.

That night it rained. All night long. At five a.m. when the girls went out to retrieve Cloudy, he was soaked. The blanket was so wet it was heavy.

Meanwhile, the van had arrived to take Cloudy to the show. Lisa Savino undid Cloudy's buckles, and pulled the bright red blanket off of him.

Underneath stood a hot pink pony.

And with his heavy coat he was very pink, very noticeable. What were they going to do? The van was already waiting. They loaded the pony and they went to the show.

And there, in the short stirrup division, one pink pony, with several very fat braids, competed.

Some people will do anything to get the judge's attention.

# BEGINNER'S LUCK

# ⌐∴ ALIADAM

The doctor always wanted to be involved in horse racing. His dad loved the races, loved to bet them, to watch them. So it was in his blood. But he wanted more than that. He wanted to be part of racing, to stand in the winner's circle with his very own horse.

The doctor grew up watching and listening to his dad playing the races. When he got old enough, he played the races himself. The education stood him in good stead for he became a strong student of bloodlines. He learned which sires produced sprinters, stayers, or broodmares.

He was watching, waiting, for the opportunity he knew would show up. One day it did. He knew that Hasty Road, although himself not a sire of runners, was a phenomenal sire of broodmares who could *throw* runners. Hasty Road had sired a mare, Bayberry Road, who would be running in a $5000 claiming race.

This was the break the doctor had been waiting for.

He placed a call to his lifelong friend, Richard Sinrod. The two had talked about becoming partners on a racehorse for years. "There is no reason a horse like this should be available in a $5000 claiming race," he explained to Richard. "This is our big chance. Do you want to go in with me?" he asked.

Richard did, and the two arranged to have the horse claimed.

When a horse is claimed, the original owner may claim it back if the new owners keep it racing. The only way to insure this doesn't happen is to retire the horse. So Bayberry Road, although only five, was retired.

That was all right: her role was to become a broodmare.

Now they just needed to find the right stallion.

The doctor is a surgeon in New York City, and one of his patients owned a stallion named Anticipating. The horse was one of the leading sires in Maryland. The doctor felt that the combination would be a good match, and Bayberry Road was sent off to Maryland to be bred.

She "settled" very nicely, becoming pregnant and then returning to New York to have the foal. By doing this, the doctor and Richard insured that the foal would be considered a New York bred, and thus be eligible for numerous purses available specifically to New York breds. In order to maintain eligibility, Bayberry Road would then have to be bred back to a New York stallion.

Bayberry Road gave birth to a strapping bay filly. She was named Aljadam, an amalgam of the names of Richard's, and the doctor's, children. Aljadam left home as a two year old and went to a farm in North Carolina for schooling. She was taught to run, how to break from a gate, and the general rules of the road for a racehorse.

She returned ready to start her racing career.

The first hurdle a racehorse has to get over is obtaining a "gate pass." The horse has to prove that it can successfully break from a starting gate. Once it proves this, it is then awarded the pass. No horse may enter a race until it has that pass.

Aljadam passed her first test.

Now the challenge was to get her entered in her first race. This is not such an easy task. Trainers (and owners, if they're involved) need to consider how the horse has been training, and what type of horse it seems to be. Does the horse appear to be a sprinter? Or, is it better at longer distances? Does it favor dirt tracks or turf?

Even when you find a race that's right for your horse, it doesn't necessarily mean you can get in. For any race with say, 10 starters, there are often as many as 25 who want to start. So, Aljadam couldn't just be entered in the first race that was chosen for her.

Horses have to draw for their spots, and if they're lucky, they get in. If they're not lucky they don't, but those that don't draw in, get "stars" so that they have priority the next time they draw for a race. Horses with stars can get into a race before the draw, and the more stars they have, the more priority.

It gets more complicated. In order to try to accumulate these stars, trainers will often enter their horse in a race that they don't want them to run in, for example they may enter a dirt horse in a turf race. Then they hope that the horse doesn't draw in so that they can accumulate a star for a more suitable race. If they *do* draw in, and then scratch, they don't get a star.

All in all, it took five months to get Aljadam entered in her first race. Three days before she was due to run, she fractured her leg.

Aljadam was out for six months before resuming her training. Meanwhile, the doctor had switched to a new trainer, Nat Krohn. He chose Nat because the man was a real horse lover, someone that he felt was good for the horse, and that he and Richard could work well with.

Finally, Aljadam was sound and entered in a race. She came in fourth, bringing in some money for her owners, trainer, and jockey. Her owners were thrilled.

In Aljadam's second race, she came in third.

These third and fourth place finishes were not only encouraging, but lucrative as well. Aljadam was winning purse money, plus she was bringing in additional money in breeder bonuses as a New York bred.

The placings also paced the filly's progress suitably. Had Aljadam won, she would lose her maiden status and have to move up, encountering more challenging competition as she did. So placing, yet not winning, worked out well for everyone.

Meanwhile, Richard and the doctor, along with their families, were getting to know their filly. She was easy to be around, and quite a character. When Aljadam was in the saddling area, she picked up the routine very quickly. She knew her legs were going to be stretched, so why wait? She did it herself. Anyone watching Aljadam at that point would hardly believe their eyes as they witnessed the filly doing her own pre-race yoga routine, leisurely stretching each limb before she was led out for her race.

Aljadam ran under some rather untraditional silks. Reflecting the outlook of her owners, Aljadam's jockeys wore gray silks with a yellow smiley face on them.

In her fourth race, Aljadam won. She won big. Running only at major tracks such as Belmont and Saratoga, Aljadam was in the money for 13 out of her 21 races. Soon, she was "black typed". When this happens, the horse's racing history is shown in darker type in the racing program. It means that the horse has come in in the money in a stakes race. A horse who is black typed has made it into the big leagues of the racing world. (only one percent of racehorses make it into this category)

Richard says that he always knew when Aljadam was going to win a race, because she would look him in the eye before she headed for the starting gate. "This one's mine," she seemed to say.

As Aljadam proved herself a competitive horse, her owners felt more and more sure about their choice of Nat Krohn for a trainer. With a competitive horse, a trainer needs to be particularly careful because if it ends up in a race where it is over its head, it will literally kill itself trying to win.

Aljadam won so much for her owners that Richard was able to set up trusts for his two daughters. One trust sent his daughter Alysha through college and two years of vet school, as well as putting his other daughter Amanda through college. And that was only Richard's half of the money!

The greatest thrill the mare gave her owners was on a Sunday, Father's Day, at Belmont. Aljadam won the featured race. It was a Father's Day her owners will never forget, and it was made even sweeter when the doctor won the Pick Six (meaning he picked the winners of six races in a row designated as the "pick six").

The odds of someone winning a Pick Six are very remote. But the doctor obviously knows how to beat the odds. How else could you explain how two neophyte racehorse owners won stakes races and a small fortune at the top tracks in the country, with a homebred horse?

# ↔ DAKOTA

**B**arbara could barely contain her excitement. Her daughter Patty's first client was about to arrive.

Patty had been riding for a large part of her life. Starting at nine with her first pony, Patty rose rapidly through the ranks. By 11 she had already won the Pony Medal award by winning nearly every pony medal class she entered. And she did this while riding against kids who were much older.

At 13, she qualified for both the Medal and Maclay finals with her equitation horses. At 15, she qualified for Harrisburg, Washington, and Madison Square Garden with her very fancy junior hunter Royal Prospect. The duo came home with ribbons from all three shows.

Patty always looked the part. Her attire matched her ability. In her custom boots and finely tailored jackets, Patty looked like a model for equestrian wear.

Things didn't change when Patty went off to college. She competed on her intercollegiate team, winning the top award, the Cartier Cup, at the Finals. Patty rode on the team for two years. It was no coincidence that for both of those years the team won the IHSA National Championship.

School vacations were not vacations for Patty. She purchased a young Thoroughbred to bring along while she attended college, and showed him during Christmas break and summer vacation. She and First Flight qualified for Harrisburg and Washington in both the Amateur-Owner and First Year Green divisions.

But now Patty had graduated and it was time to start her professional career. The only horse in the barn was the talented First

Flight. It was time to add a customer.

Barbara anxiously awaited the arrival of the trailer. All the time, money, and energy she and Patty had spent were about to pay off.

Patty had gone to pick up the horse, Dakota Star. His owner, Alicia, had tired of him and he was now just a backyard ornament. A teenager, Alicia had become more interested in school and boys than the horse.

The trailer arrived, and Barbara hurried over to check out the new star.

Her heart sank.

He looked about as wide as he was tall. His blue roan coat hadn't seen a curry in ages, a thick, wiry mane draped to his shoulders and the feathers on his feet would have done a Clydesdale proud. The little mutt had whiskers so thick he looked as though he had stuck his nose in a porcupine.

"Oh my God," thought Barbara, "From Madison Square Garden to *this?*"


Dakota had been purchased by his former owners as a western trail horse. They were new to horses and had not consulted a professional about the purchase. So Dakota had problems. The western trail horse didn't go western and he was way too spooky to do trails. He had come to Patty to be trained and sold.

Unlike Barbara, Patty was elated. It was her first customer. Someone was going to *pay* her to train their horse.

Patty started riding Koty. He hadn't been doing much and needed a refresher course. Patty worked with him daily: grooming him, clipping him, riding him, and lavishing him with care and attention. Then she started jumping him. She found he liked the ring: he seemed to feel secure in it. And he loved to jump. She called her Mom to come watch him jump. Barbara still wasn't impressed. "Yeah, whatever," she thought.

Patty tried him on trails, but that proved disastrous. Koty spun and backed and snorted at everything, positive that horse eating monsters lurked behind every tree and rock.

The ring work continued to improve, so Patty placed an ad for the little horse in *Newsday*, the major Long Island newspaper. Koty was now jumping around little courses.

Two women responded. They wanted a horse that they could share and they came to take a look at him.

They liked him; he was cute. And his wonderful personality won them over. A real people horse, Dakota took to them immediately.

The two prospective owners were curious as to how the horse would go at a show. They asked Patty if she could take him to an unrecognized show the next day so they could see how he handled it, and so their trainer, John Strumph, could take a look at him.

Patty agreed.

Barbara, watching as Patty schooled Dakota at the show, was amazed. He looked rather cute, all fat and shiny and braided up.

It only took one class for Koty to prove his ability. Marching around as though he'd been doing this his whole life, he blew away the competition. And not only was he steady and honest, he could jump! His knees were up around his eyeballs and he was round as a ball.

Barbara met Patty as she left the ring. "You can't sell this horse!" she said emphatically. "He's adorable!"

John Strumph thought so too, as did the two prospective owners. They called that night to say they wanted him.

"His owner decided not to sell him," Patty told them.

Instead, Barbara and Patty became co-owners of Dakota Star.

Dakota went on to win everywhere in both the adult amateur and children's hunter divisions. He was reserve champion in the children's hunters at the prestigious Hampton Classic Horse Show, as well as topping the Long Island High Score awards for several years. It didn't matter what show he was in, or who was on his back, he won. With every rider he had and whatever zone they were in, he invariably qualified for zone finals.

His adorable white face and splashy body have graced the cover of a book (Hallie McEvoy's *Horse Showing for Beginners*). Dakota finished his career by taking young riders to victory in the short stirrup division. He is now a retiree in Patty's barn where he will be cared for for the rest of his life.

And Barbara will never judge a book by its cover again.

# THE NAME GAME

## THESE ARE ALL NAMES OF HORSES WHO ARE NOW, OR HAVE BEEN, IN THE SHOW RING.

What do you name the most perfect pony you've ever seen? The one who moves cute, has exquisite manners, is adorable, whose ears are always forward, and who will never put a foot wrong no matter what child you put on his back? *Learner's Permit*

Choosing a good name for a Paint or pinto is always a challenge. How about *In the Spotlight, Benjamin Moore, Color Guard, or Save My Spot?* Or, when the pinto has a roan tinge to it, he becomes *Fading Colors.* Other Paint names include *Paint by Numbers, Paint the Town, Picasso,* and *Color Me In.* An especially loud Paint is *Bravo.*

It's one of those horses you absolutely did not plan for, who somehow climbed on your trailer when you weren't looking: *Out of the Blue*

You're tired of men who don't call back, who are rude, inconsiderate, and not easy on your eyes. Your eye-catching, well-mannered horse is *My Perfect Date.*

You didn't buy a van when you retired. You bought a horse. His name is *My Kids' Inheritance.*

A small roan pony is *Bite Size.*

A small white pony is *Mr. Softee.*

*Daisy May* is her name. Your husband says that means Daisy May jump, or Daisy May not.

A dun with a lot of really dark points would be *French Toast.*

Or your Dad always wanted a Porsche. Instead, you are sitting on *Daddy's Money*.

You can always tell a Star Wars fan by the horse they ride: *Jedi Knight, Obi Wan Kenobi, Luke Skywalker, Chewbacca,* and, of course, *Yoda,* have all made appearances in the show ring.

A cute little pale chestnut pony would be *Triscuit,* a big round chestnut would be *Cheddar.* And a chestnut with a rosy tint to it? *Peaches.*

If you bought your daughter an adorable chestnut pony mare, she would be called *Sugar Plum Fairy.* Also adorable in pony size is *Adorabelle.*

Many of us have horses so we can have some *Time Alone.*

And many of us feel that our horses are our *Kindred Spirit* or *Soulmate.*

More breeds have become "acceptable" in the hunter ring, but when the Appaloosa Scandal was showing, it truly was a bit scandalous. And *Something Shocking* apparently made the judges do a double take as well.

What better name for an Appaloosa sprinkled with white spots than *Connect the Dots?* A leopard Appaloosa aptly named is *Dropcloth.*

A chestnut pony mare who has to stop and admire herself every time she goes near a mirror can be no other than *Vanity.*

A beautiful palomino mare with flaxen mane and tail and perfect socks would no doubt be *Malibu Barbie.*

Your good friends Harry and Adria Diel gave you the dressage horse you'd been drooling over. You named it *Whattadiel.*

Not with your spouse? Your horse is *My Alibi.*

Roans get a bit of a twist with *Aroan Again* and *Leave Me Aroan.*

If your horse is a star in the jumper ring, good names would include *Air Jordan* and *Frequent Flyer.*

And if your horse's sire is *Seattle Slew*, then you might name the baby *Slew the Coop.*

If your horse is an easy keeper, *Air Fern* fills the bill. And if she's a hard keeper, she would be *Ally McBeal.*

Big body, big head: *Mike Tyson.* Or *King Arthur.*

If your Thoroughbred's registered name is *Whereforeartthou*, his barn name would have to be *Romeo.*

You're a writer, and you own a draft cross. You would name him *Heza Rough Draft.*

Anyone who has ever owned a cranky pony will understand *Will if I Want To.*

If you love candy and own a black and white pinto, what else would you call it but *Good N Plenty.*

A red and white pinto would aptly be called *Red Beans and Rice.*

Small ponies by design need to be ridden by young riders. So it's no surprise that they come up with names like *Winnie the Pony, Nimbus 2000, Daddy Said So,* and *Toys R Us.*

And this one we can all relate to: If your first horse was *Checkbook,* the next one would undoubtedly be *Overdraft.*

# LIfe Has its ups and DOWNS

# ⤳ Little Star

L ife has its ups and downs, but some years it feels more like a roller coaster.

The show year looked promising. Betty Oare already had an elegant Thoroughbred gelding, Micanopy, who had been purchased from Scott and Kara Hofstetter, to show in the amateur-owner hunters. He had been named for a little town located between Gainesville and Ocala and was light on his feet and a lovely jumper. But Betty wanted another mount, so her relatives were out horse hunting for her.

There was Stolen Moment, a chestnut mare, who had been spotted by Betty's husband, Ernie, when he was judging Lake Tahoe. And there was Estrella (Spanish for Little Star), who had been found in California by Linda Reynolds, Betty's sister-in-law. Besides being a very good jumper, Estrella was cute and reminded Linda of Micanopy.

Both horses looked very promising. Bucky took a look at them first, and told Betty she needed to try them.

Betty went to Lake Tahoe, where she watched Leslie Steele ride Stolen Moment, who was competing in the first year greens at the time. She liked the chestnut mare a lot. Then she headed to Santa Barbara to see Estrella.

Estrella, belying her warmblood background, was very refined. The Dutch cross by a Holsteiner stallion was very springy, like a little ballerina. Too springy, perhaps. Betty thought, "If she's this bouncy on the ground, can I stay with her in the air?"

She could. When she went ahead and tried Estrella over a few fences, she was pleased to find the mare very easy to jump. And she loved her lightness. The bay mare felt as though she "had wings on her feet."

Estrella was in the stable of Mary Gatti, a California trainer, and Patrick Stanton was showing her in the second year green division. Patrick got on her while Betty watched her jump. "Very impressive," she thought.

Which one should she get, she wondered? She returned home just in time to pack her bags and leave to judge in Cincinnati for five days. Meanwhile, Ernie made the decision for her. They made offers on both horses.

Both were accepted. In a joint family effort, while Betty judged, Ernie put together the paperwork on the horses and arranged to have them flown to Baltimore. Their son Morey picked them up at the airport and trailered them home to Virginia.

For their first show with Betty, Stolen Moment and Estrella went to Blowing Rock Horse Show. Each was wonderful despite the dreadful weather. It was rainy and foggy, not the sunny California skies Estrella was accustomed to. Yet, with Morgan Thomas riding, she was champion in the second year green division.

Estrella quickly proved to be not only a star, but also a very special pet. She became so used to Bucky spoiling her constantly with treats, that when she didn't get them her face would take on a very pitiful look. Betty teases that someday, Estrella is going to stop mid-course and go to Bucky on the rail in search of goodies.

Things were really shaping up. Betty's horses were winning at all the big shows, with Estrella bringing home the circuit championship from Ocala. Then Betty went to Culpeper. It was August, 2002.

Getting ready for the Amateur-Owner division, Betty and Micanopy were jumping in the schooling area. Landing from a jump, they tried to go around a turn at the end of the ring. Unfortunately, there was a person walking their horse on the rail going the other way. They tried to pass each other but didn't quite make it. Betty's foot caught the other girl's stirrup, breaking her ankle and catapulting her into the air. Landing on her arm, she broke her shoulder in the process. The pain was horrible, the worst pain Betty had ever suffered.

The one bit of luck that came Betty's way that day was when her boot had to be removed. She knew she had to take it off because her ankle was swelling rapidly. Luckily she had had the good fortune to put her bigger boots on that morning. She escaped without having to suffer the horrendous fate of watching her custom boot being cut off her leg.

Betty spent three days in the hospital, and when she got out, her new right ankle was constructed with a plate and five screws. Her right shoulder and arm were in a sling.

One thought dominated Betty's mind. She was qualified for Washington. Could she be ready?

Ten days later, the initial cast was taken off of her leg and Betty began getting around with a walking boot and a walker. A week later she was working with a therapist, Helen Ritz. Helen, a friend's daughter, knew that Betty had a time frame in her head, and she knew that Betty was determined.

Jointly, they accomplished the goal. Betty is quick to give credit to Helen, who knew just how much to push and just what Betty needed to do. And Betty did it. She worked hard. Five a.m. would find her at therapy, pushing her body, pushing her mind to their limits, to accomplish her goal.

When the doctor okayed it, Betty was back on a horse. She felt good. Washington was coming.

For two weeks Betty rode anything she could. Bucky had been keeping the horses fit and schooled and they were ready. Was she?

Betty hadn't jumped a course in two months and Washington was just around the corner.

She and Estrella jumped a cross-rail. So far, so good. They jumped a vertical. Then an oxer.

That was it. No need for more. They were ready.

In their first over fences class at Washington, Betty and Estrella were the winners. She and Stolen Moment were second. Estrella ended up Grand Amateur-Owner Champion, as well as taking the championship in the working division earlier in the week with

Sandy Farrell. She and Sandy had also taken the championship in the workings at the Capital Challenge.

When Betty and the horses returned from Washington, Betty checked the standings. Her bay mare with the small patch of white on her face was in the race for Horse of the Year. "Let's go for it," Betty thought. They went to the Duke Benefit Horse Show, where they were champions. They were on their way. The National Horse Show was only two and a half weeks away.

Returning from North Carolina, it was dark when she and Ernie arrived home. Their yard, which is constructed in graduated heights, has stone staircases connecting one level to the next. Betty, carrying her suitcase, proceeded very cautiously, protecting her bad ankle. But she misjudged in the blackness and left out a step, crashing down onto the ground. She screamed in pain and in disappointment, sure that now her good ankle was broken.

It wasn't. It was her fifth metatarsal, on the outside of the foot. Betty was back in the hospital.

She called an orthopedic surgeon, a friend of hers. "I guess there's no way I can ride again in two and a half weeks?" she asked dubiously.

"Well, maybe," he replied.

After taking x-rays, he put Betty in an air cast. Then it was up to her.

She was the *best* patient, icing her ankle and keeping it elevated as often as possible. Eight days later the cast was off and Betty's ankle was taped up. Four days later the big question remained. Would Betty be able to ride?

Dressed in tight paddock boots which helped lend support to the ankle, Betty got on her hunt horse and rode. She jumped a few crossrails. "I can do this," she thought.

Walking was another matter. She used crutches, determined to protect her ankle.

Then, shortly before the National, Betty's mother suffered a stroke. Betty forgot about the show, thinking only of her mother's health.

Betty's mother rallied.

Betty and Estrella did compete at the National Horse Show, galloping around the perfect footing of Wellington's Grand Prix field. The beautiful forward course showcased pace and brilliance. There were bending lines and many individual fences. It was ridden off the eye and Betty and Estrella were in their element. The mare was a star, galloping easily around the course and jumping brilliantly, clearly enjoying herself as much as Betty. The fences were works of art, the brush and walls beautifully garnished with flowers, contrasting with the rich green of the field.

Betty had no problem riding. She did have trouble jogging for soundness. Upper level hunters who are in contention for a ribbon have to jog back into the ring, led by their riders, after their round to prove they are sound. Estrella was fine, but if the judges had been watching *Betty*, they would have failed the jog.

The glamour was back at the National. Hunter exhibitors entered under the bridge where all the big jumpers came in for their grand prix classes. There was brilliance and pizzazz, with crowds of spectators filling the stands and reminding many of the days when the garden attracted that kind of a turnout.

Betty and Estrella were Grand Champions in the Amateur-Owners, and Estrella outdid herself in the victory gallop, clearly playing along with the music. And with that victory they clinched the title for Horse of the Year.

Estrella's win was celebrated on the night before New Year's Eve. Horse people, friends, neighbors, doctors, and anyone who had helped Betty through her comebacks, were invited. Over 350 people enjoyed the music and dancing, the fabulous food, and the videos of Betty and Estrella's winning rounds at the National. In the festive atmosphere, the struggles were forgotten. Everyone kicked up their heels and toasted Betty and her very special bay mare for a well deserved victory.

Betty didn't get to attend the USA Equestrian awards dinner, didn't get to accept Estrella's Horse of the Year award. While she was at the convention she learned that her mother had taken a turn for the worse. Betty returned home to be with her Mom who passed away shortly afterwards. The loss hit Betty hard, for the two had been very close.

Betty's mom knew, however, that her daughter and the horse Estrella, overcoming major hurdles, had earned the coveted Horse of the Year award.

# ⤳ Victory Tour

He looks big but he's not really. In size that is. But in heart Victory Tour is as big as they get.

Richard Sinrod already had a horse, one he had purchased for his daughter, Amanda, to ride. But Richard grew tired of watching his daughter ride. He wanted to try it himself.

He started taking lessons on horses at the barn. Like most of us, it didn't take long until he was totally hooked. Riding school horses was not enough. He wanted one of his own.

Richard went to a lot of trainers. He looked at many horses. But they weren't suitable. He was just beginning to ride. Why, he wondered, were they showing him horses that were more than he could handle? He started to realize that perhaps there were good reasons that horse dealers often had a reputation akin to used car salesmen.

At River Run Farm in Brewster, New York, Richard was shown Victory Tour. Janet Meizels, a trainer from North Salem, took him to see five horses. All were reasonable prospects.

But it was Victory Tour who grabbed Richard's attention. Perhaps, Richard says, it was "Vic's expressive, beautiful brown eyes, eyes that truly give you a look into Vic's heart and soul." And, "It was uncanny that their color was identical to the eyes of my Swiss Mountain Dog, Kevin."

The horse was owned by Rhonda Dretel, a woman who loved and pampered him to the point of rubbing him down with a special recipe of baby oil and talcum powder. But she was tiny and had recently injured her back, and Vic was a powerful horse. He was too much for someone with a bad back, and besides, she had decided to focus on dressage. Vic was a handsome and athletic horse, but he would never be a star in the dressage arena.

So, Victory Tour was for sale.

He was seven years old, a three-quarter Thoroughbred, one quarter Percheron cross. Although he actually measures under 16.1 hands, his big bones and muscular build make him seem far bigger. People are often fooled into thinking he is closer to 17 hands.

Vic went with Richard to Long Island for a week long trial. He never went back to Brewster.

He did accompany Richard to Vermont for a while, where they trained with Gwen Perkins. Gwen had been an upper level event rider for years before giving it up to settle down and have a family. One ride on Vic convinced her to get back into eventing. She even tried to convince Richard to sell her the horse, sure that Vic could bring her back into the sport in a big way.

Richard was happy to have Gwen ride, and event his horse. But sell him? No, the handsome bay with the blaze face had in record time become a family member. And the horse was so talented, and so kind, that Richard, who had only been riding about six months at the time, starting doing some beginner level events himself.

Vic did well with Gwen at events in Vermont and Massachusetts, including Stoneleigh Burnham. But his eventing career was cut short when Richard and Vic returned to Long Island.

There aren't too many events on Long Island, and Richard and Vic needed something else to do. Richard had a friend who suggested that he might enjoy hunting. The friend hunted with the Smithtown Hunt.

Richard had never tried hunting. Neither he nor Vic knew what to expect on their first hunt. When they arrived, Richard noticed a little uneasily that everyone was wearing goggles. He couldn't imagine why. He soon found out.

Hunting on Long Island bears little resemblance to hunting in Virginia or upstate New York. There isn't much in the way of open fields or beautifully groomed lanes. Hunting on Long Island means galloping through underbrush, mowing down small (and not so small) trees, ducking branches and hoping to come through it all unscathed. As Richard and Vic flew through the thickets, Richard thought that goggles were beginning to make a lot of sense.

Richard did not manage to come through unscathed. Scratched by a branch he couldn't avoid, he ended up with blood spilling from the bridge of his nose. He continued riding with one hand. The other one was holding a handkerchief against his nose to stop the bleeding.

Vic could easily have taken off with Richard, gone around jumps, or done pretty much as he pleased. He didn't. His rider was injured, so he took over. He took over by doing exactly what he was supposed to do, following along with the field and jumping the jumps. It was the first inkling Richard had of what he had on his hands: a fabulous hunt horse. Vic had a new career.

Vic appeared to understand hunt protocol, keeping up with the field but not overtaking the master. Watching him, you would have thought he'd been hunting his whole life.

When they came to a stop, Marge Smith, a long time member of the hunt, noticed the bleeding newcomer and came over to have a look at him.

"Well," she observed, "I don't think it's broken and it won't need stitches." So, "Welcome to hunting!"

Victory Tour always finished a hunt and every time he went out he ran in first flight. His rider was, without fail, his first concern. He was never lame. In fact, Vic was such a great hunt horse that in three years time Richard was offered his "colors": a pink coat. This honor generally takes quite a while to achieve, and Richard is quick to credit Vic. The horse was so well respected and liked in the hunt field that it was Vic, more than Richard, who earned the pink (actually scarlet) coat.

People who had hunted their entire lives and rode alongside Vic often remarked that he was one of the best hunt horses they'd ever seen.

Once, when they were hunting in Southampton, there was

a very nasty looking fence that all the horses were stopping at, some of them throwing their riders in the process. Richard watched all the refusals and thought confidently, "Vic will jump it. Vic never stops."

Richard had his back to the fence and didn't notice the man who had been ahead of him attempt to jump it. The man's horse stopped, dumping his rider over the fence, where he landed in a heap.

Richard turned around and pointed Vic at the fence. As they approached it all seemed well until they were right at the base of it. Suddenly, Vic came to an abrupt halt and made a sharp left turn. Although Richard managed to stay on, he smacked his leg against the fence, breaking his ankle in the process.

Disappointed that Vic had stopped, and in pain with his aching leg, he wondered what had happened. He had been so sure Vic would jump.

Had Vic jumped the fence, he would have landed on the man lying on the other side. He would definitely have injured him badly, if not killed him. Vic had not stopped because of the ugly fence. Always careful of his humans, Vic had refused to land on one. He was saving a life.

Vic didn't only save physical lives. He was good at emotional rescues, too. When a friend of Richard's, Alicia Maguire, lost her father in a freak accident, Alicia was devastated. Her mother had died when Alicia was nine. She had no brothers or sisters. Now her father was dead. She wasn't sure she could survive. Grief consumed her. The thought of getting up in the morning and getting through the day was overwhelming. Alicia didn't know how she could get through this.

Vic was the answer. Richard offered Alicia the opportunity to ride him and she took him up on it. The honest horse with the kindest eyes gave Alicia a feeling of security that she sorely needed at the time. In return she showered him with love.

Men, Alicia felt, often don't give horses the love they need, Men often think of them like a motorcycle: turn the key and it goes.

So Alicia was giving to Vic what she felt he wasn't receiving from Richard. And Vic gave to her what she wasn't otherwise receiving from life. Vic seemed to understand her sadness and he responded generously.

Alicia's love for Vic helped soothe her grief. The work she did with him, teaching him tricks, such as how to bow, gave her an outlet, something to focus on besides her loss. Alicia says that "Vic was always there for me," and "I will never, ever forget him. He is a very dear horse to me."

Alicia also tried to provide balance to Vic's life. The work he did for Richard was strenuous, galloping and jumping in hunts and hunter paces, and going for trail rides that lasted for hours.

So Alicia worked him lightly. Together they went for relaxing trail walks, taking in the beautiful scenery of Old Westbury. She would spend time just playing with and cuddling him. Vic learned to cuddle back, to give kisses. He would bow for a treat, for the apples and carrots that Alicia brought in bushels. He learned to tolerate fly spray and Show Sheen, something he would never allow coming from anyone else.

With Alicia caring for him, he shone like never before. In the sunlight, he glittered so brilliantly that sunglasses were required equipment in his presence.

Alicia says that Vic's attitude is always "I'll do it." There is never any hesitation, only an honest desire to please his rider. And for Alicia it wasn't so much about how well Vic performed. "That," she says, "was what Richard did." For her it was the love and trust, the emotional bond between them.

When Richard retired from his law practice, he and his wife Yael made a decision to leave Long Island. They moved upstate to Millbrook, New York, an area famous for its hunts and its horses. Vic took to the Millbrook Hunt readily, and the terrain that was far more welcoming than Long Island's. Initially, they "capped" with Millbrook. To join a hunt, one has to be invited. It wasn't long before the invitation came. Once again, Richard gives Vic the credit. "I'm still not sure whether it was me or Vic who was actually invited."

Vic and Richard also competed in the numerous hunter paces in the area. Vic treated hunter paces the same way he ran in hunts. He always brought his rider home in one piece. Often, Vic would hunt one day and hunter pace the next, with no ill effects.

Vic also loved to take trail rides, with Richard's dog, Kevin, coming along. If Kevin dropped out of sight, Vic would stop, turn his head a little, and wait until he saw Kevin reappear. The two developed a very close bond, and out of it came a logo that Richard designed, featuring Kevin pulling a carriage while Vic took a well deserved rest in the comfy seats of the vehicle. At the reins was Richard and Yael's cat, Crayons.

One day a particularly long and arduous hunt lasted nearly three and a half hours. When it was over Vic and Richard still had a 50 minute hack back to the barn.

Vic seemed all right when they returned.

But the next day, when the groom went to walk him, Victory Tour, the horse everyone called "The Ironman," was dead lame. He didn't want to put any weight on his left hind leg.

The prognosis was poor. Dr. Michelle Ferraro of Millbrook Equine Veterinary Clinic diagnosed a high suspensory injury. She told Richard it looked like the end of Vic's career.

Richard was horrified. He wasn't about to give up so he asked what could be done. He was told to put Vic on stall rest and then to hand walk him.

So Vic lived in his stall for quite a while. Always the gentleman, he never complained. Then he was moved to a nearby barn where he had a stall which was attached to a small turnout area. He could move around a little himself, and Richard hand-walked him every day for three months.

When Vic didn't get any better. Richard became more worried.

He shipped Vic to New Bolton for a second opinion, Unfortunately, the opinion was the same. The horse's career and riding days were over.

Richard, thinking the horse was in pain, made a heartbreaking decision. He told them to put him down.

But he was surprised by a call from the New Bolton vets asking him to reconsider his decision. They had all fallen in love with the kind horse with the big blaze face. And no, they didn't feel that he was in much pain.

To say that Richard was relieved would be a terrific understatement. If Vic wasn't feeling that badly, then they could keep trying.

The next move was to send Vic to a farm that did racehorse rehabilitation. Vic stayed there for a year. It wasn't the country club, no swims and Jacuzzi™ sessions. Just blistering to try to increase the circulation and improve healing.

But after a year, Vic was still lame.

Richard couldn't believe it. He was desperately hoping something would work.

"I give up," he thought. He didn't want to; he loved the horse. But he didn't know what else to do.

So Richard bought himself a new horse. And Vic was sent to be retired on the farm where the new horse had been purchased.

Richard thought he had done the right thing. Vic had been so good to him, such a blessing in his life. He says, "I was so lucky to have had Vic as my first horse!"

He hoped that, since Vic was not in pain, giving him a good retirement would be a happy ending for him.

That didn't seem to fit with Vic's plans. It wasn't too much later that Richard was hunting in the area where Vic lived. Dropping by the barn, he was shocked at what he found. Vic was grossly underweight, had bite marks all over his body from the other horses, and his feet were abscessed from standing in deep mud.

This was not what Richard had had in mind for a comfortable retirement. In two minutes, Vic was loaded on his rig and headed back to Millbrook. Here he was stabled with Richard's new trainer.

Oddly enough, this trainer had had a jumper who had suffered the same injury as Vic. The jumper had had surgery at New England Equine and was now back in the show ring.

The trainer urged Richard to have the same surgery done on Vic, and she didn't have to do any arm twisting. This could be the solution Richard had been looking for.

Dr. Bradley did the surgery, a bone marrow transplant. It wasn't too much later that an ultrasound showed that the injury was completely healed.

But while Vic's health was improving, Richard's wasn't. One day when he had returned home after riding, he was unloading some manure from the bed of his pickup for the garden. Suddenly he found himself in horrible pain. His eyes hurt, his teeth hurt, his jaw, his back, even his hair hurt. He couldn't imagine what was happening to him. He called Yael. "Come straight home! I think I'm having a heart attack."

Then he called 911. He was found flat out on the lawn, phone still in his hand, unconscious. Raced to Vassar Hospital, suffering from a burst aneurism, his chances of survival were almost non-existent. The doctor told Yael not to expect him to make it. He didn't think that Richard would come out of the six hour operation alive.

Richard fooled them. He survived.


Vic slowly regained his fitness, after years of inactivity. His trainer, and her students brought him along a little at a time.

Step by step Richard came back, too. Watching the kids ride Vic, watching his horse come back from surgery, gave Richard the inspiration to come back himself.

"If he could do it, I figured I could do it too."

While Vic was walked, and then trotted lightly, Richard would take five steps in the ring. Soon Vic was up to trotting more, cantering some. Richard made it to once around the ring, then three times. Horse and rider came back to life together.

Vic began his new life, a life he spends mainly with kids. Not wanting the weight of adults on Vic's back, Richard decided that only kids (or petite adults) could ride him.

Once again, Victory Tour takes charge on the hunt field. Again, he shows everybody how it should be done. One year eight kids hunted Vic: seven were awarded junior colors. The following year, five kids in the hunt earned their colors. Four of them had been riding Vic.

Vic competes in hunter paces, too, and it was at a hunter pace where Richard (riding another Percheron/Thoroughbred cross, aptly named Moose), ran into Rhonda Dretel. Rhonda said that selling Vic was "the only mistake I've made in 14 years."

Rhonda had found Vic in Maryland, and said it was "love at first sight." She, too, was taken by his big, kind eye.

Rhonda had started hunting, riding with a pack in North Carolina.

Since Rhonda was riding in hunts, a light bulb went on in Richard's mind. "How about a reunion?" he thought. He invited Rhonda up for the next weekend to hunt with him: on Vic. They would ride with the Rombout Hunt.

Rhonda eagerly accepted. "Vic was exactly as I remembered," she says. "Just as handsome at 21 as he had been at seven."

And hunting him was "just amazing." He's such a "good-hearted horse, he makes it so easy, all you have to do is just sit there and look pretty."

She was thrilled that she got to experience the Rombout Hunt on Vic. The hilly territory of Dutchess County, New York, is very different from the sandy, flat, terrain of North Carolina, and this particular hunt was "wild." At one point they were galloping down a blacktop road. Vic didn't care. Rhonda says he makes you "fearless. He's got a lot of guts and a lot of spirit. And he just carries you through."

Rhonda hadn't ridden Vic in 14 years when she hunted him with Rombout. When she dismounted, she gave Vic a cookie. He gave her a kiss. She cried.

Vic does a lot more than hunts and hunter paces. The kids at the barn also ride him in lessons and shows. In a recent show at the Dutchess County Fair, Vic and his petite rider Sierra Rothwon

179

four first place ribbons in huge classes. They also took home the Perpetual Trophy for their division. All day long people came up to find out if Vic was for sale. Vic was the perfect child's horse, and there wasn't a person watching who could fail to see that.

Everyone from the barn said, "No, no, sorry, not for sale. Not ever. No chance." Their "noes" weren't convincing enough to the crowd of possible buyers. That is, until Richard's wife Yael gave the final answer.

"No, Vic is not for sale. Ever.

I'd sell Richard first."

# ⟶ A fine Weekend

**K**aren Amedeo and Beverly Vars were going away for the weekend. Karen's daughter Kelsey had qualified for the Intercollegiate finals, and Karen wouldn't dream of sending her off to such a big event on her own. She attended all of her daughter's shows and was her biggest fan...and oftentimes groom!

Kelsey rode for Stonehill College, a small school located in Easton, Massachusetts, and she had qualified in the open (hunt seat) division, the highest level that the intercollegiate system offers.

But Karen and Beverly weren't just going for the horse show. Karen had asked Beverly to come along for an escape weekend, time for two longtime friends to shop and eat and explore together. They were going to check out the Grand Old Opry, eat at great restaurants, and sightsee and shop. They were planning a fine weekend.

They had hardly gotten started when things began to go awry. At the airport, security refused to let Beverly through because the imaging system had detected nursing scissors in her handbag. These were not just any scissors. They were Beverly's first pair of nursing scissors, something that every nurse treasured.

And security wanted her to throw them out! "No way!" thought Beverly. She was *not* going to throw them away. Yet their plane was leaving very shortly. It looked like it might be leaving without them. What could she do?

Digging through her carry-on bag, Beverly found a folded overnight bag. She pulled it out, chucked the scissors inside, and checked it in. They boarded the plane.

"Okay, just a small hitch," they thought, "now it's on to our big adventure."

Arriving in Tennessee, they proceeded to their hotel. There was, however, a larger hitch. It seems that there was no room for them.

They had made reservations: all of the Stonehill team had made reservations for this hotel, the Holidome. But somehow Karen and Beverly's reservation seemed to have disappeared. There was no room.

Tired from their trip, they were in no mood to beg for a room. But, after considerable negotiating, they got one. It was a handicapped room, with a bathroom almost as big as the bedroom. It faced the back of the hotel with a prime view of the dumpsters. But it was a room.

"We're horse show mothers, we can deal," they told each other.

Karen sank on one of the beds and picked up the TV remote. She was beat. It was going to feel so good to relax and just zone out with some television.

She pushed the button. Nothing happened. She pushed it harder. No response. The remote didn't work.

Meanwhile, Beverly flicked on a light switch. No light illuminated the room. The bulb was burned out.

They looked at each other.

"It's okay, it will get better," they told each other.

When they went to use the bathroom, the toilet didn't flush.

Too tired to deal with the problems of the room, they fell asleep. Things would get better tomorrow. They just knew it.

Beverly and Karen woke at 6 a.m. in order to go watch the show. Beverly was looking forward to starting her day with an invigorating shower. The steamy water felt good against her skin. Then she noticed that it was also rising above her ankles. Water was filling the bathtub. The drain didn't drain.

That was all right, though. Management had told them they would be moving to a new room that day, the room that should have been theirs originally.

Well, maybe not. A call to the front desk was anything but reassuring. The room they were going to move to, the one that they had originally reserved, had only one bed. Well, they would have to deal with it later. They had a horse show to get to.

At least at the show, things were going well. The stadium was gorgeous. The new $20 million Miller's Coliseum had just been completed and the Intercollegiate Nationals were lucky enough to be the first horse show to use the new venue.

Bob Cacchione, along with the sponsors, personally made the presentations to the winners. Bob was the founder of the IHSA. Everyone received an award as it was an honor just to be there. After a class finished, those that did not place were called forward individually and presented with a beautiful "participant" ribbon, ribbons that were every bit as nice as the winners'. All participants also received an embroidered duffel bag.

The big intercollegiate players were all here: University of Findlay, St. Lawrence University, Mt. Holyoke, Virginia Intermont. Little Stonehill, despite being Reserve Champion in the Zone 1 regionals, was not even considered a contender.

A big contingent of parents and supporters had arrived to cheer on the Stonehill team. The school may be small in size but its team spirit is unsurpassed.

Today they were off to a great start. Tom Brennan won his Intermediate over Fences class. The team was inspired. What a great way to begin Nationals! The kids were all enjoying themselves. The pomp and ceremony of the show with its Parade of Teams and award presentations made them realize they really had earned their place in the spotlight.

And Stonehill, little underdog Stonehill, stood in third place at the end of the day!

Karen and Beverly didn't leave the show till nearly 10:00 p.m. So much for the partying they intended to do that night. They were tired. They'd have to delay their fun until tomorrow night.

As they were driving back to the hotel, the weather started

turning ugly. Wind whipped small branches around their rental car as they approached the Holidome and the sky looked threatening. Listening to the radio, they heard severe weather warnings.

They reached the hotel safely, glad to be back. Visions of freshly made beds and big fluffy towels beckoned them. The visions vanished as reality greeted them instead. The beds were just as rumpled as they had left them that morning. The same soggy towels lay on the bathroom floor, and the bathtub was still ankle deep in water.

They looked at each other. They were getting tired of complaining. The room with one bed wasn't going to work. They weren't asking for much. All they wanted was a clean comfortable place to sleep and shower. Things were not getting better.

Still, they *were* horse show mothers. They could cope. They found the hotel laundry, helped themselves to clean sheets and towels, and made up the beds themselves.

At the horse show, however, things did keep getting better. Shannon Tibbits, a freshman, started out Day Two with a Reserve Championship. Then Sarah Muller, a sophomore, won the Championship in the walk-trot-canter class. Karen's daughter Kelsey continued adding to the score by taking fourth in the Open Flat. Coach Sheila Murphy had done an excellent job preparing the kids, and it showed.

Stonehill was now, miraculously, in the lead.

Tonight they had something to celebrate, and celebrate they did! Karen and Beverly went to the Opryland hotel where they treated themselves to a lavish dinner. Crab cakes, steak, braised asparagus, baby green salad, some nice wine. This was more like it. This was what they had come to experience. And, to top it all off, it was served by a handsome waiter.

The hotel was mammoth, so large that five football fields could have comfortably fit inside. And it was so designed to make you feel as though you were outside, right down to a river running through the building. One could take a riverboat cruise on this river, and Karen and Beverly did, blissfully unaware of what was brewing outside.

That changed as soon as they opened the hotel door. A howling wind greeted them, and rain splattered the building.

The weather had gotten markedly worse. The wind constantly tried to blow their little rented Neon off the road, and whipped branches and unidentified objects across its hood and roof. It took forever to get home. Karen could barely keep the car on the road. The weather reports were ominous.

The one blessing was that when they returned to their room, it was made up.


Driving to the show Sunday, they learned that tornadoes were headed their way. Skies were black, it continued to rain, and the wind was strong again.

But the show eclipsed all worries about the weather. It was a cliffhanger. The outcome would be decided by the last class of the day. If Centenary's rider placed first or second and Stonehill's Dyanna Rucco scored no points, Centenary could win. If Findlay won the open fences and Centenary earned no points, Findlay would be reserve.

Findlay's ride won. Centenary's rider had a refusal. And Dyanna Rucco got the nod for Reserve Champion in the Open Fences. That made Stonehill the National Champion Intercollegiate team.

It was time to celebrate! Kids, parents, and coaches from all of the teams headed to Nashville, to the Long Horse Saloon where they danced the night away. It was a marvelous celebration for a wonderful win.

But after the party they had to get back to the hotel.

The weather was worse than ever. Torrential downpours were whipped in all directions by powerful winds. Everyone was scared. Getting the cars back to the hotel proved to be a herculean task.

Karen and Beverly were not surprised to find their room unmade. They got some clean towels and figured that was the best they could do. All they had to do now was glance at each other.

"We're horse show mothers, we can deal," was unspoken.

Exhausted, everyone fell asleep quickly.

But, not for long.

At 3 a.m. the phone rang. Karen answered it. It was the front desk. "The hotel is directly in the path of a tornado. Evacuate your room immediately!"

Throwing ragged sweaters over their nightgowns, the two women fled the room. They had been told to go to the Grand Ballroom, where there were no windows.

Since they had been in the handicapped room, Karen and Beverly were the first ones to be alerted. So they were also the first to arrive in the Grand Ballroom.

Both registered nurses, they threw themselves into action and began making phone calls. Every room had to be called. They called coaches, students, parents. Evacuate *now*! And knock on your neighbor's door and yell as you're leaving.

Despite the fear, they couldn't help but be intrigued by the phone list. Beverly is a top trainer herself. She and Karen found themselves calling some of the most well-known and well-respected trainers and riders in the country.

As they made the calls, Karen and Beverly were also answering the switchboard, taking frightened calls from worried parents who wanted to know if their kids were all right.

As bad as things were, Karen did see some humor in the situation. Here was Beverly Vars, who was one of the classiest, most gracious women Karen knew, in her nightgown, barefoot, making phone calls in the middle of the night. Minus her glasses, which had been left behind in the hasty exit from her room, she had had to borrow a student to read the room numbers in order to make the calls. And in the middle of the mayhem, suddenly water was pouring over Beverly's head. Part of the roof had blown away and the water just tumbled right in.

As the kids came in, they were directed to take shelter under the tables. It was ironic how the parents and coaches arrived frantically, without thinking to bring anything useful with them. The kids, on the other hand, showed up with blankets and pillows; some of them even had their hard hats on. One of the most prevalent dangers from a tornado is being hit by flying objects, and these kids, thinking ahead, were protecting their heads.

Some of them were so exhausted and apparently unperturbed, that they went right to sleep under a table.

Karen and Beverly found themselves amazed by the scene that took place before them. At the show grounds, the riders and coaches were competitors. Here, everyone banded together with one common goal: to protect the kids. The coaches and remaining parents (many had already left for home) went from table to table, not seeking shelter for themselves, but making sure the kids were protected.

Soon, water was not just coming in from the roof, but pouring up through the floors.

"What does a tornado sound like?" someone asked Karen, who had spent some time living in the south.

"Like a freight train," she replied.

"Like that?" she was asked, as a tremendous roaring engulfed the hotel.

The ceiling shook, the walls shook, and people huddled in terror.

But again, scary as it was, the scene was not without some relief. Looking around, there were hundreds of people, many of them famous coaches and riders, all in their pajamas, huddled under tables: all in this together. Stock seat riders, hunt seat riders, dressage riders, from big schools or little schools. Their differences were forgotten, they were all united by a need to survive a storm.

And survive the storm they did. As did the horses, who were fine in their stables at the Coliseum.

The world was a different place when they emerged. Oranges, thousands of them, decorated the grounds of the badly damaged hotel. The tornado had plucked them from trees in its path and deposited them in piles at the hotel. The indoor pool had turned itself inside out and now a river ran through the hotel from the force of the eruption. Lawn furniture from the outdoor pool lay in twisted shapes all around.

There were planes to catch. Returning to their rooms, Karen discovered that a watch and bracelet she had brought with her had been stolen during the evacuation. Shrugging it off, she went to take a quick shower before they left.

She reached for her shampoo and conditioner. They, too, were gone.

They were only too happy to get on their plane.

Their planned fun and frivolous weekend had come to an end...or so they thought.

Six weeks later Karen received a bill from Dollar Rent A Car for $6458 for hail damage to the rented Neon. When she had returned the car, it had been inspected and no mention of hail damage had been made.

Karen checked with all the other parents; no one else had been billed for hail damage, yet the cars had all been in the same parking lot.

Karen had kept her return slip for the car. When she contested the bill Dollar sent her a copy of the slip.

It had been altered.

# AND MORE...

# CRISCO

The mousy brown pony itched. Itched terribly. In fact he itched so much that the only thing that made him feel better was rubbing against a tree…continually. The problem was, you could reach just one side at a time, and both sides itched. So no matter how much he could make one side feel better, the other side still drove him crazy.

Then he happened upon the perfect solution. A tree nearby had sprouted two trunks that grew nearly parallel to one another, with just a very small space in between.

The pony squeezed in between the two trunks. Now, both sides could be scratched at the same time.

It was perfect.

He started rocking back and forth, in order to scratch better. Rocking forward, his ribs compressed, letting him get further between the two trunks. But as his ribs cleared the space, they expanded back to their normal width. There was no going back. There was no going forward. He was wedged between the two trees. Stuck.

The pony's owner looked out his window and started when he saw the little Shetland cross stuck in a tree, hung up between his rib cage and his hips. He didn't know what to do. How could he rescue the pony? Call the fire department and tell them his pony was up a tree?

Instead he called a landscaping company. He thought if they cut one of the tree trunks down, the pony could be freed.

He called a vet too. The vet's receptionist answered the phone, and wasn't sure how to respond to the call. "Your pony is stuck in a tree? Could you give me a little more detail on that?"

The owner explained that he had already contacted a landscaper, and that he wanted the vet to sedate the pony so that it wouldn't panic when he cut down the tree.

So the vet went out on the call, a little hesitant, a little unsure of what she would find.

It didn't take her long to locate her patient. She surveyed the situation and quickly figured out what had happened.

Now the question was how to undo it.

She could see immediately that cutting down one of the trunks was not the way to go. They were good size trunks, about eight inches in diameter, and if one fell, it would surely crush the pony.

She and the pony's owner might be able to push him out. But that was risky; the pony could easily get hurt in the process.

Looking up, she could see that the tree opened up a bit more above where the pony was. If they could get him up a little higher, that would help. But they needed something else too. They needed the pony to be slippery so he would come out easily.

It didn't take her long to come up with a solution. Perhaps it was her background as an event rider that made her think of it, for she was familiar with the practice of smearing Crisco on horses to enable them to slide over jumps if they hit them. So it was Crisco they would be needing.

She asked the pony's owner if he had any. He disappeared into his house, and it was quite some time before he resurfaced, carrying a disreputable looking can of Crisco that had probably been sitting in his pantry since the 1970's. Whatever, it was still greasy and that was all they needed. The vet grabbed handfuls of the goo and slathered the pony up. He was covered in grease when the landscaper arrived.

She could see that it took every ounce of self-control that the man had not to burst out laughing. A tree with a greased pony sticking out both ends was not something you came across every day.

The vet, the landscaper, and the owner all grabbed the pony's chest and front legs and lifted him up higher, freeing his rib cage from the two trunks.

Then, one, two, three, *GO!* Together they gave a big shove. And *pop*, out popped the pony from the tree.

No fireman ever rescued a kitten from a tree better.

# ⤵ THE OLD WESTBURY HORSEMEN'S FOUNDATION

The village of Old Westbury on Long Island has a rich heritage: a heritage largely based on horses. The Old Westbury Horsemen's Foundation was started to preserve that heritage.

It was founded in 1977. The major purpose was to keep the trails open to riders, and to preserve those trails for succeeding generations, to continue the village's equestrian legacy.

Unfortunately over the years, along with the trails, the Foundation deteriorated. Fewer riders were taking part and it was becoming more of a social club than a club dedicated to its original mission.

John Shalam saw what was happening and decided to do something about it. He became involved with the organization about 12 years ago, and soon became president. At that point many of the trails were rather neglected: some were lost entirely, others had become too overgrown to be usable.

The treasury, too had been neglected, for it was precariously low on funds.

John changed all that. He brought in new blood and raised money, revitalizing the organization. He went to the village board of Old Westbury itself and enlisted their help. John says he was fortunate in that "the village of Old Westbury's trustees are very enlightened." They respect the history of the village and thus it was arranged that whenever an estate is broken up, the Horsemen's Foundation is granted a ten foot perimeter around the estate for riding trails. This continued the tradition of the original charter.

The village is "extremely supportive." What turned out to

be a bit of a surprise is that developers have often been quite supportive as well. Many of them love the idea that the village is equestrian oriented and are very willing to comply, as they feel that it adds to the value of the community.

The trails serve not only riders, but walkers, too. What better way to work off an evening meal than to take a walk on exquisitely beautiful trails surrounding your neighborhood?

In addition, the trails act as a buffer zone, preserving the rural atmosphere and beauty of the village.

John not only brought the Foundation's focus back to equestrian pursuits, he also reversed the sad state of the treasury. He raised funds by emphasizing Old Westbury's heritage. One of the biggest fundraisers is a picnic held yearly at Old Westbury Gardens. The event features demonstrations by the Nassau Suffolk Rough Riders, the Smithtown Hunt, and stars such as Neal Shapiro, a former member of the United States Equestrian team.

An information booth is located at the picnic, providing visitors with information about the Old Westbury Horsemen's Foundation, and promoting equestrian life in the village of Old Westbury.

A journal put out by the Horsemen's Foundation, regarding the day at Old Westbury, also raises a lot of money. The journal relates the history of the Foundation and Old Westbury, lists the events that will take place that year, and also gives some background information on Old Westbury Gardens, the site of the event. Advertising space is sold for the journal, and between this, dues, and donations, the treasury is quite healthy and funds are readily available for maintaining the trails.

Another important project that the Foundation has undertaken is developing an insurance policy to protect homeowners. With lawsuits so prevalent these days, it was necessary to insure that homeowners were comfortable with allowing riding around their properties. The policy has worked extremely well.

The Foundation realizes that a good relationship between riders and residents is crucial. They work hard to be sure that anyone using the trails uses them responsibly, and any complaints are handled immediately.

As a result, residents, village trustees, and homeowners all share a good relationship and respect what each contributes to the community as a whole.

A dedicated and very capable group of horse people now run the Foundation, as John stepped down a few years ago. He is quick to credit Marty Sternberg, who took over as president, with doing a wonderful job of continuing the Foundation's mission. Marty is ably assisted by Yigal Tropp, who takes care of membership and maintains the trails, Judie Chessin, who is the secretary of the organization and helps hold the whole thing together, and Eric Schwartz, the treasurer.

Besides the miles of trails throughout the village, the Old Westbury Horsemen's Foundation also has hundreds of acres open to them through the State University of New York at Old Westbury, and C.W. Post College. Dr. Calvin Butts, President of SUNY allows them to ride on his campus' 600 acres, while President David Steinberg of C.W. Post (Long Island University) lets them use the trails on his grounds.

The Foundation maintains all of its own trails, as well as the trails it uses on the campuses, and on additional trails which run through Muttontown (where a 400 acre equestrian park is located) and through Brookville. Many people find it amazing that Old Westbury is only 25 miles from Manhattan, yet it has a vast system of riding trails.

To further preserve Old Westbury's past, John, Marty, Yigal and two other friends from the Foundation purchased the Old Westbury Equestrian Center, which is located on 27 acres managed by Marty Sternberg. The Center boasts barns, paddocks, a magnificent indoor arena, and, of course, access to the miles of beautiful trails of Old Westbury. John feels that the center adds to the tradition of maintaining horses in Old Westbury.

John and his partners do take the time to enjoy the paradise they helped save, meeting every Saturday and Sunday at 9:30 a.m., weather permitting, to go for a ride through Old Westbury's unique trail system.

Riding trails throughout this country have been destroyed, or are being threatened, due to the growth of housing developments. Fortunately, there are men like John Shalam and Marty Sternberg who have the vision to see what is happening, and take the necessary steps to stop it. The Old Westbury Horsemen's Foundation, along with the trustees and residents of the village of Old Westbury, have preserved a rich tradition. Thanks to them, this wonderful way of life, rooted in Old Westbury's past, is forever a part of its future.

# ⸙ Next Thursday

There's an old riddle that goes,

> "A man left town on Thursday.
> He came back on Thursday.
> But he was only gone three days.
> How is that possible?"

Tina Stephenson's son Shane was born on a Thursday. So was her daughter, come to think of it.

When Tina and Shane went looking for a horse for Shane to show in the jumpers, the search proved quite exhausting. But finally they found the right prospect. On a Thursday. The bright chestnut gelding was a Quarter Horse who had been a barrel racer. He was 15.3, compact, and cute. He was fast over the fences, catlike in his agility.

So they had him vetted, on a Thursday.

He passed the vet, and Tina went to deliver a check on a Tuesday. But she couldn't find the woman she needed to pay. She tried again on Wednesday. Still no luck. Finally on Thursday, she was able to hook up with the horse's owner, and deliver the check.

The former owners weren't sure when they could deliver the horse. They would call and let Tina and Shane know. And they did. It was on...Thursday.

Since everything kept happening on a Thursday, Tina and Shane began to question what would happen Next Thursday. And so, Next Thursday became the name of the new horse.

He proved perfect for Shane. Tina showed him just once, and he was so easy that she handed the reins to Shane and said,

"He's all yours, go show him."

He did, starting in the 2'6" jumpers for a very short time, then moving up to the three foot division. The first year Shane and Thursday were together they were overall champion in the jumpers for the Old Salem horse show series.

But soon Shane outgrew Thursday, in more ways than one. Not only was Shane becoming physically too tall for the horse, but his riding skills were outstripping the horse's scope.

So once again Tina and Shane went shopping. And once again it seemed to take forever. It got to the point that they began to feel desperate. There were certain requirements. The horse had to be big bodied enough to carry Shane's rapidly growing frame. Tina wanted a Thoroughbred, for the intelligence and quickness inherent in the breed were just what she wanted in a jumper. And she wanted a horse with mileage, one who knew its job well enough to cover up when Shane made mistakes. Yet with all these requirements it still needed to be affordable. So, Tina was willing to settle for a high maintenance horse to allow for flexibility in the price.

Still, no horse...

Tina told everyone to be on the lookout, to let her know if something suitable for Shane became available.

Still no horse.

Finally, they said yes to one that Tina tried to pretend would work. In her heart she knew it wouldn't do. The horse was vetted. But his blood work proved unusual, indicating something amiss in the liver. They decided to wait and retest the horse to make sure it wasn't just a false reading.

The very next day, a Thursday, the phone rang. It was a call about a big chestnut Thoroughbred that sounded like just what Tina and Shane were looking for. They made plans to go see the horse. When they got there, in no time they knew he was the one. They were thankful the other horse hadn't worked out, for it would have been disastrous.

They immediately put a deposit on the horse.

The day was...Thursday.

And the answer to the riddle is:
"He was riding a horse named Thursday."

# ‿᷄ SECOND CHANCE

Little Joe was cute. And he was fine for Erica's first horse. But he *was* little. The chestnut with the big white blaze stood a mere 14.1 hands. His sweet temperament and great ground manners were perfect for someone just learning the ropes around horses. He did not have a lot of training, but he was fun to ride.

The woman at the barn had assured Erica that in less than a year she and the young horse would be wiping up at the shows. She told her that Joe was the perfect horse for Erica and they could learn together. But the woman lied. Like too many horse dealers she wanted to make a sale without considering the appropriateness of the match. And Erica, and her mother, Sue, were new to horses. They were trusting someone else's opinion, someone they thought was competent.

So they bought Little Joe. Erica enjoyed him. He loved to trail ride, and even Erica's mother could get on him.

But things started to fall apart at the barn where they kept the horse. The woman who ran the place couldn't be trusted; she had lied once too often to Erica and her Mom. It was time to find a new place to board.

Erica had been taking lessons from a man at the barn, Ike, who had moved to a stable not too far from where they lived. They followed him. Things were much better at the new barn. Jim, the owner, was honest and did his best to be sure the horses were well cared for. He was knowledgeable and Erica and Sue felt that they could trust his advice.

Erica and Little Joe started taking lessons. Then Ike quizzed Erica about her ambitions. The advice that followed was something she didn't really want to hear. Little Joe wouldn't cut it. His small stature and limited stride would not allow Erica to pursue her dreams in the show ring. He was also too green. Ike was honest with her. Erica needed a horse with more education, one that could help her learn. Ike said he would let her know when he became aware of one that suited her needs.

Meanwhile, Erica alerted her best friend Nikki to keep an eye out for a new horse. The search was on. Just a few days later Nikki called, all excited. A handsome ex-racehorse had arrived at the barn, his mane braided as though he had just been to a show. This could be Erica's new horse! Ike took a look at him and thought he would be suitable. He was a good size for Erica, with plenty of stride.

The second she saw the horse, Erica wanted him. She couldn't wait to ride him, she was so excited! Ike took her into the office, and showed her the information about the horse, whose racing name was "Call Me Later." His race record was included as well as a note from the woman who had owned him. She called him "Private Malone" and she had retrained him as a hunter/jumper. She'd taken him in some shows and he had done well.

That night Erica rode the new horse in her lesson. He was *so* different from Little Joe! At first Erica had a hard time adjusting. The horse's stride was huge, and it was hard for her to sit his canter. But she loved him. He was athletic and willing and she knew they could make it work.

Anytime she was around the new horse, Erica's eyes shone. She brought her Mom and her boyfriend, Tyler, to see him. For a week she rode him, getting to know him, and the bond between them started to develop. He still wore his braids, as everyone thought he looked very handsome in them. One day Erica decided it was time to take them out.

As she was undoing the braids, Erica dropped her scissors. Leaning against the bay gelding's hind leg, she bent over to retrieve it. Something hard and powerful slammed into her stomach. Thrown down the aisle by the force of the impact, Erica landed in a heap, her arms wrapped protectively around her stomach. Sue,

Tyler, and Nikki rushed to her, terrified at what had happened.

Sue screamed to no one in particular, "*Get someone!*"

Erica would not move her arms from her stomach. "Let me see," Sue said. Erica refused. "Erica, I need to see how badly you're hurt." Erica shook her head. She didn't want her Mom to see because she was too scared to look herself. What had the horse done? Why had he kicked her?

Finally she let her mother look. A big scrape crossed her stomach which was rapidly turning violent shades of black and blue. Sue breathed a little sigh of relief. She'd been afraid that Erica had had her scissors in her hand and had gotten stabbed by them. Still, she didn't know how badly injured her daughter might be. Erica was loaded into the car and Sue rushed her to the hospital.

As they waited in the hospital, Sue firmly told Erica "You're *never* going near that horse again!"

Erica didn't reply.

Her father met them at the hospital, and while Erica was being examined she could hear her parents arguing. It upset her. Erica didn't understand what had happened, but she did know she wanted the horse. There was something special about him. He and Erica were going places, she knew that. But how would she sway her parents? How would she convince them that the horse deserved a second chance?

The doctors told Erica that she needed bed rest for three days, and was not to ride again for a week. That night she discovered how narrowly she had missed the operating room. The doctors had found blood in her intestine. Luckily, they found only a small amount and so she was spared going under the knife.

Erica wanted the horse known as Private Malone desperately; Erica's mother did not. When Erica told Sue her feelings, Sue told her firmly, "You're keeping Little Joe, and this horse is going to the glue factory."

Jim, who owned the horse, was in the middle. "Take as much time as you want to decide," he told Erica. "I'll hold the horse for you." Jim wanted to be sure the horse was right for her. He didn't want anyone getting hurt, nor did he want anyone stuck with a horse they weren't happy with.

People told Erica she was crazy. "What do you want *that* horse for? He could have killed you." Erica knew the horse hadn't meant it. He wasn't vicious. Something had provoked him. Two days after she was kicked Erica went back to the barn. She felt fine now and she told her Mom she wanted to go check on the horse.

"Don't go near him," Sue told her.

Looking for Erica a little later, Sue found her in the stall, talking to the horse. "I know you didn't mean it, you didn't mean to hurt me," Erica was saying.

Ike pushed her about the horse, telling her she should buy him. He thought the horse was safe, and he proved it by riding him without incident and then by throwing things at the horse, trying to get him to react.

He didn't.

Two weeks later Erica bought Private Malone. Although Sue wasn't happy about it, she knew it was what Erica really wanted.

It took her a while to feel comfortable about picking up the horse's hind feet. Even now she gets a bit nervous when he's dancing around. Tyler, the world's best boyfriend, often picks them out for her.

As happy as Erica was with her new horse, one thing worried her. Every few weeks, the bay gelding would go lame on his left hind, the leg that he had kicked her with. It wasn't too bad and it would go away, but what if he got worse once he started to work harder, what if he couldn't show?

And always in the back of her mind, and in Sue's, was the nagging question, what had made him kick her?

They consulted several vets, tried different shoes, still the horse continued to go off. Then, a massage therapist was called in. When she did some exploratory work on the horse's left hind, she narrowly missed being kicked herself. She had hit a trigger point, a very sore area on his leg, an area that needed careful massage work. That was why he had kicked Erica. She had inadvertently caused him pain, he reacted in self defense, and unfortunately got Erica in the process. Mystery solved.

Erica and her new horse have been together a year now. The horse has blossomed, his ribs and backbone covered now by over 100 additional pounds of muscle and fat. His once dull coat now gleams. Their hesitant first steps at horse shows have become confident now, as they become more and more a team. They may not always get a ribbon, but, as Erica says, they always have fun together and the bay gelding "always does his best for me and he always loves me, no matter what." When horses and people have faith in each other, wonderful things happen.

Things aren't always what they seem on the surface. To judge anything, be it a person, animal, or situation without knowing all the facts, is unfair. We need to give things the benefit of the doubt, to give what Erica gave when renaming her horse, a "Second Chance."

# ⟿ Unforgettable

Carrie Hutton got the opportunity of a lifetime, an opportunity that most of us only dream about. The owners of a fancy Russian warmblood named "Unforgettable" were looking for a rider for their horse.

This wasn't just any horse. He was a beautiful mover, a horse who cracks his back over the jumps, and is gorgeous to look at. This horse could go places. The wonder of it all would be that he would be Carrie's to ride and she didn't even have to buy him!

His owners, the Arute family, loved the horse, but he was a bit of a challenge for them. Though very talented, he was green, and was rather insecure when it came to jumping. He needed someone to give him mileage, somehow who could provide him with the confidence that he lacked within himself.

At the Farmington Horse Show in Connecticut, Lori Arute ran into Leslie Hutton (Carrie's mom). She introduced her to Carrie. Carrie is a very accomplished rider and Lori wondered, "Would she hit it off with Unforgettable?"

Carrie could barely believe her luck. One look at the horse and she was in love. He was eight years old, a bay with just a tad of white on his hind legs, a long neck, and a pony face that made him not only unforgettable but irresistible.

When Carrie rode him they clicked immediately. Unforgettable (whose barn name is Spencer) could sense her confidence, and Carrie loved riding him. She knew she was on something special, a horse that was probably more talented than anything she'd ever sat on. Yes, he was green and nervous, but with time and patience things would change.

Carrie had complete freedom with Spencer. The Arutes

trusted her and let her do what she wanted. Basically they just said "Here you go, do what you want, and we'll just come to the shows and cheer you on."

It couldn't get much better.

Carrie and Spencer went back to square one. The horse was living at The Pines in Glastonbury, Connecticut, and he and Carrie worked with Cammy Wheat. They took a lot of lessons, and their first goal was just to trot over ground poles. Spencer didn't want to trot, he wanted to canter through them. It was a big accomplishment when he finally relaxed and trotted through the ground poles.

When Carrie and Spencer started jumping, Spencer was a little nervous about going to the jumps. He wasn't entirely sure that that was what he wanted to do. It was this nervousness and insecurity that had prompted the Arutes to consult Carrie in the first place.

Yet they had faith in their horse, as did Carrie. A lot of people didn't. They would see Spencer being spooky and nervous, and didn't think he would ever go anywhere.

For six months Carrie and Spencer trained at the Pines, taking baby steps. The baby steps were progress, and led to bigger accomplishments.

At Spencer's first few shows, he would stop because of something silly, like a hose he spotted lying on the ground outside of the ring. Carrie was patient with him, never pushing him, but letting him understand that there really wasn't anything to be afraid of. He grew to trust her, and the next major accomplishment came when Spencer jumped all of the fences the first time in the ring. The confidence that Spencer felt in Carrie was spilling over into his performance.

Carrie says, "That was awesome." The faith that she and the Arutes had in the horse was beginning to be rewarded.

For Carrie, it was wonderful to experience the day to day progress. "The feeling one gets from working with a young horse, bringing it along, and coming together as a team is part of what makes life worth living."

Finally, Spencer became a hunter rider's dream, the kind of horse on whom you can just loop the reins and let him carry you over the fence.

Along the way, Carrie and Spencer picked up a lot of awards. Competing in the Adult Amateur Hunter division in 2004, the two of them were either Champion or Reserve in nearly every show they entered. At Lake Placid, out of over 40 competitors in their division, she and Spencer earned two seconds.

Carrie was thrilled, and made plans to take Spencer to the Middleburg Classic, in Virginia. Then she picked up a prize list for the Westbrook Horse Show. Something caught her eye.

The prize list stated that the horses who earned champion and reserve in her division at the Westbrook show were automatically qualified for the National Horse Show. Plans changed. They went to Westbrook instead.

At Westbrook, the first day's competition took place indoors. She and Spencer took a first and a second over fences. The next day, when their classes were held outdoors, they won both over fences classes, and took a third in the hack class.

It was a no-brainer. They were qualified for the National Horse Show: champions in the younger division of the adult amateurs and Grand Champion Overall for the division.

The National Horse Show, which has undergone many changes in the past few years, is now split into different locations. Carrie and Spencer qualified for the New York City location, held at Pier 94. It was called the Metropolitan Horse Show.

Carrie was amazed at how far they had come. She says, "It's awesome being given the opportunity to ride a horse like this, and bring him along, and then to have something so good come out of it." She's extremely grateful to the Arutes for giving her the ride on Spencer, and for becoming such special friends.

Besides being Spencer's first competition at the National, it was also Carrie's. It was a major test for both of them.

The location of the horse show, a pier in New York City, is

hardly a natural spot for horses. It was very busy, right in the middle of the city, and as Carrie was unloading Spencer from the van, taxis and traffic were speeding by. She was very proud of him; he didn't let the commotion get to him at all.

The schooling ring was tiny, and always chock full of horses. They were so jammed in they seemed to be going around like a hack line, head to tail. Schooling was allowed in the main ring (at 4 a.m. for Carrie's division), but with 100 horses in the ring at one time, it was hard to accomplish anything.

It was, Carrie says, "an awful lot for a green horse to handle." You could tell from the look on Spencer's face that he was wondering, "What on earth is this all about?"

Carrie herself was feeling a bit overwhelmed.

At the show, Carrie and Spencer were helped by Scott Stewart. He had been watching Spencer come along, and said he was very pleased with the progress the horse had shown.

When it came time to actually compete, Spencer was still a bit spooky and unnerved. But he did jump around...like the green horse that he was.

In their flat class, they placed eighth. In their second class over fences, Carrie and Spencer had settled in nicely. Carrie was so excited to be at this show, so appreciative of the opportunity that she had been given. She was thrilled when they came ninth, for just pinning in this prestigious event was an honor. Spencer was competing against horses with vastly more experience than he had. Two years previously, he wouldn't even jump if circumstances were a little suspicious. Now, here he was jumping around in a stadium in New York City, with crowds of people surrounding him and the blare of traffic in the background.

Carrie believed in Spencer, and Spencer believed in Carrie. That belief took them all the way from baby steps to the big time.

We're already planning our next volume. If you've got a story you'd like to share with us, let us know! It can be any breed, any discipline. We'd love to hear from anyone, from Arabians to Icelandics to warmbloods, from driving to endurance, racing to eventing to reining and everything in between, including the family pet! Contact Ann at annjamieson23@gmail.com.

*Photo: Debbie T. Kilday*

# Ann Jamieson

Ann Jamieson is a USEF judge licensed in hunters, equitation, and jumpers. She writes for *Today's Equestrian* magazine, and competes her horse Fred Astaire in hunters and First Level dressage.

Ann lives in Connecticut with her amazing Ocicat, Hobbes.

CPSIA information can be obtained at www.ICGtesting.com
Printed in the USA
BVOW08s0318240713

326733BV00008B/75/P

9 780977 250561